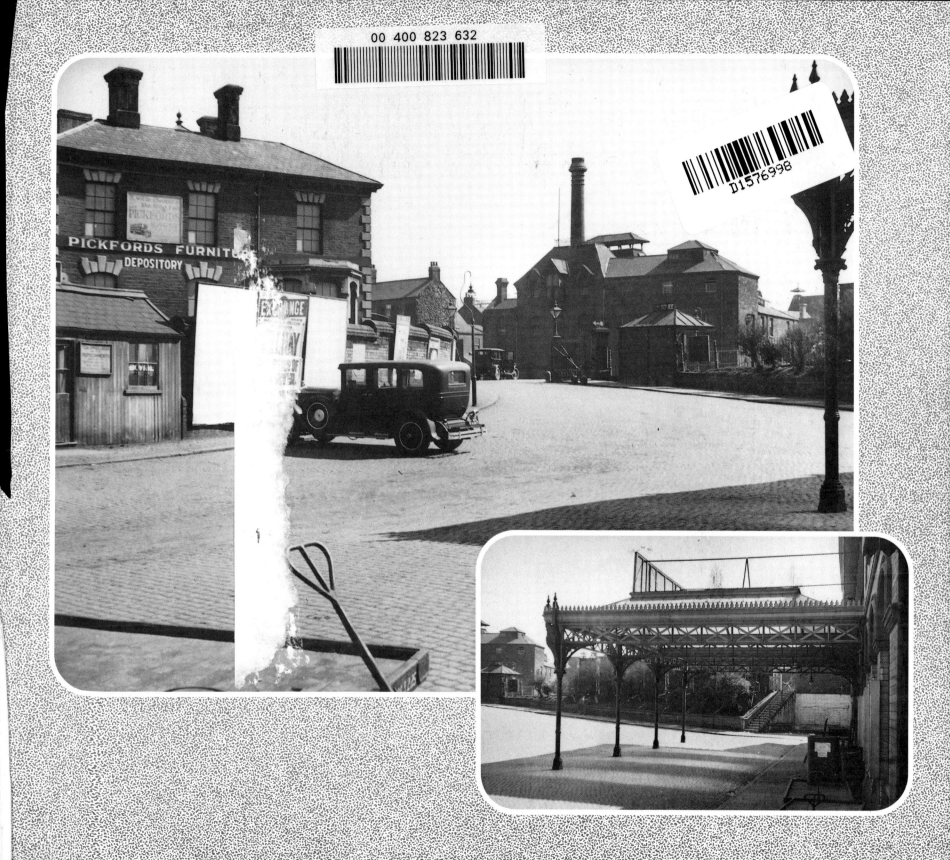

RAILWAY IMAGES
AROUND NORTHAMPTONSHIRE

Frontispiece. Dwarfed by the massive proportions of Stanier Coronation Pacific No. 46250 CITY OF LICHFIELD, a commuter glances nervously at the steam emanating from the locomotive's inside cylinders as he heads up platform 1 at Northampton Castle Station, March 1960. (*L.H. Cummings*)

RAILWAY IMAGES
AROUND NORTHAMPTONSHIRE

by

RICHARD COLEMAN and JOE RAJCZONEK

W. D. WHARTON
Wellingborough

First published in 1992 by
W.D. Wharton
37 Sheep Street
Wellingborough
Northamptonshire NN8 1BX

ISBN 0 9518557 1 9

Designed and typeset by John Hardaker, Wollaston, Northamptonshire
Printed and bound in Great Britain by
Woolnough Bookbinding Ltd
Irthlingborough, Northamptonshire

ACKNOWLEDGEMENTS

We are indebted first and foremost to all the many photographers who have so kindly allowed us access to their photographic collections, to John Meredith for the loan of his father's negatives, to Ron Cadman for details and photographs of the Daimler Railcar, to A. Scott for the loan of photographs from the N.B. Scott collection, and also to *Northampton Chronicle and Echo* for the use of their extensive negative collection. This book would not have been possible without their superb pictures.

Thanks must also be attributed to the many individuals who gave up their time to assist with information, especially Peter Butler, Brian Denny, Ken Fairey, Tony Foster, Les Hanson, David Hanson, Tony Heighton, Ian Lyman, Graham Onley, Rex Partridge, Robin Puryer, Ross Smith, Barrie Taylor, the late Victor Hatley and the staff of the National Railway Museum Library. Also many railwaymen assisted, and these include Archie Barker, Cliff Davies, Joe Hasdell, Doug Hewitt, Rodney Pearson, Ken Poole, Ray Roworth, Dave Savory, Joe Smiddy and Signalman Don Underwood.

Much darkroom assistance was provided by Steve Stringer and Victor Rajczonek, who continually produced excellent prints from the negatives, and Jess Ley provided expert retouching skills where required.

We would also like to thank John Munro for his encouragement and help in locating a publisher; John Hardaker for his continuing patience in the face of our numerous requests to alter and amend our original layout and manuscript; Mick Sanders for answering our incessant questions about laser scanning and printing techniques; and finally Robert Wharton who has given us great freedom in the choice of photographs during the preparation of this book for which we are extremely grateful.

Half title caption
St Mary's church spire in Far Cotton is superbly framed by one of the watering columns at Northampton shed on Sunday 21 February 1965. Both braziers are well topped up with coal as they burn fiercely to prevent the watering column freezing up. *(Robin Puryer)*

Title page caption
An unidentified class 8F begins to cross the Welland Viaduct at Harringworth with a northbound empty coal train returning to the Midlands coalfield during the spring of 1959. *(Tony Heighton)*

Front end-paper captions
(Left) A scaled-down version of an original Train Departures poster from Northampton Castle station, giving train movements between 9 June and 14 September 1958. *(Tony Foster collection)*

(Right) A view from Northampton Castle station into the station yard on Saturday 8 April 1939 finds an unusual taxi cab in the shape of a Belgian 'Minerva'. (Inset) A view of the ornate station canopy which was removed later the same year. *(W.J.S. Meredith)*

Back end-paper captions
(Left) Work is well advanced in removing the tracks in the cutting at Brackley during June 1968. An English Electric type 4 diesel No. D330 prepares to move off with a demolition train as the Great Central Railway comes to its sad end. *(Delmi Battersby)*

(Right) In the depth of the severe winter of 1962/63 'Jubilee' No. 45575 MADRAS leaves Brackley with the 12.30 p.m. Marylebone to Nottingham train on 27 December 1962. *(Delmi Battersby)*

CONTENTS

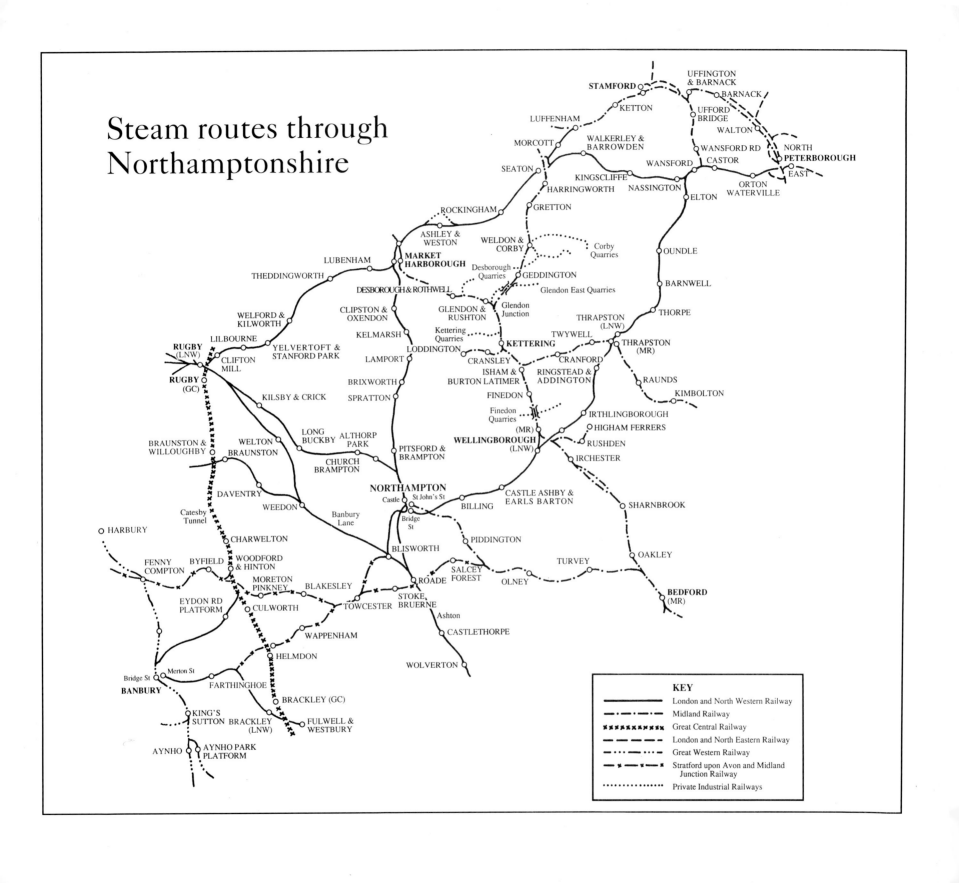

Steam routes through Northamptonshire

KEY

London and North Western Railway
Midland Railway
Great Central Railway
London and North Eastern Railway
Great Western Railway
Stratford upon Avon and Midland Junction Railway
Private Industrial Railways

INTRODUCTION

IN our two previous photographic works covering Northamptonshire railways — *Steam Nostalgia Around Northampton* and *Steaming Into Northamptonshire* — a comprehensive look was taken at the various railway lines that traversed the county, showing the variety of motive power at numerous locations along the routes.

In this third volume the chapters have been arranged to portray the many different aspects of the working railway in and around the county. Images start from the pre-grouping days of the late 1800s, but while steam dominates a majority of the photographs a glimpse of the early diesel types indicates that modernization was on the way.

The once thriving ironstone industry in the county relied heavily on iron ore being moved by rail, and one chapter shows industrial steam at its evocative best, while in another the photographers have moved away from the trackside and photographed the railway in the rural and urban landscape of Northamptonshire and its borders. People are a very important aspect of railways, and many images of workers, travellers and observers are included, showing how they were all involved.

The exciting variety of styles of railway photography by the many contributing photographers has allowed us to convey the unique atmosphere of the county's railways. The railway scene has always lent itself to creative and progressive photography, and we have tried to balance the traditional approach with the more artistic so that the complete spectrum of photography has been used.

We have not attempted to cover every corner of the county, but a wide variety of locations are illustrated, and we continue to be amazed at the number of previously undiscovered photographs that come to light, and in this work most of the photographs appear for the very first time. Looking through the many hundreds of negatives and prints has given us immense pleasure, and we hope that this latest collection of railway images will gladden the heart of many people who, like ourselves, look back on the days of steam with pure nostalgia.

Richard Coleman and Joe Rajczonek

Pre-grouping Panache

1. A rare interior view of a London and North Western Railway picnic saloon at Castle station during L.M.S. days on 21 December 1929.

These coaches were available for hire from the railway by societies or private individuals. This particular example started out as a West Coast Joint Stock 42' sleeping saloon. (*W.J.S. Meredith*)

2. One of F.W. Webb's 'Dreadnought' compound 2-2-2-0 No. 1395 ARCHIMEDES in immaculate external condition awaits departure at Northampton Castle station's platform 6 during the latter part of 1900. The Webb compounds had a reputation for rather erratic steaming and sluggishness when starting away, and were soon scrapped when George Whale became Chief Mechanical Engineer of the L.N.W.R.

ARCHIMEDES was built in June 1886 and withdrawn in March 1904, a comparatively short life for a steam locomotive.

3. At the turn of this century, Webb 'Jumbo' 2-4-0 No. 2193 SALOPIAN, of the renewed Precedent class, storms away from Northampton Castle station and heads for Euston via Roade. The train is made up of six-wheel carriages painted in the L.N.W.R. livery of 'dark claret' and 'flake white'. Rebuilt to this form in February 1896, 'Salopian' would provide another 25 years service before withdrawal.

PRE-GROUPING PANACHE

L. & N. W. RY.
Northampton Castle

4. Relatives or friends of District Engineer Colonel Hull stand for the camera in a typically stern and sombre Victorian pose on the observation platform of the engineer's inspection saloon during the late 1890s.

The saloon is being hauled by the Crewe Allen single driver ENGINEER NORTHAMPTON. *(W.J.S. Meredith collection)*

5. Another view of ENGINEER NORTHAMPTON, with the engineer's inspection saloon attached, standing in bay platform 5 at Northampton Castle station in 1900. This locomotive, a Crewe Allen 2-2-2 6' single, was built at Crewe works and entered traffic in January 1857 as No. 40 (later 42) SUNBEAM, and remained in service until April 1895 before being transferred to the engineers' department and renamed ENGINEER NORTHAMPTON. Based at Northampton, she was always kept in spotless condition and continued hauling the inspection saloon until being withdrawn and scrapped in May 1901.

PRE-GROUPING PANACHE

6. On a sultry summer's day in 1900, a down express, with steam shut off for the Blisworth stop, cruises past the water tower at the south end of the station behind a renewed Precedent class 2-4-0. The tall chimney served the boiler that worked the water pumping equipment. This equipment pumped water from the reservoirs at canal level to the tanks on top of the tower, from where it was gravity fed to the water columns on the station.

7. Awaiting passengers from the express on the previous page, a train from the East and West Junction Railway stands behind a brand new Beyer Peacock 0-6-0 No. 12, all set to depart from Blisworth to Towcester and Stratford-upon-Avon.

Standing resplendent in crimson-lake livery with panels lined black, edged each side with yellow, this would have made a colourful contrast to the lined black of the L.N.W.R. locomotives on the adjacent 'Premier line'. The very low platform was shared by the 'East and West Junction Railway' and the 'Northampton and Banbury Junction Railway'. (These two companies amalgamated with a third to form the Stratford-upon-Avon and Midland Junction Railway on 1 January 1909.) At this time the signalbox was adjacent to the Northampton branch. It was constructed in its more familiar position, behind the signal gantry on the main line circa 1910.

8. *(Left)* East and West Junction Railway 2-4-0 tank No. 5 works the 11.35 a.m. mixed train of E. and W.J.R. stock away from Towcester towards Greens Norton Junction and Stratford-upon-Avon where it is due to arrive at 12.43 p.m.

At this time the coaches were 4-wheelers in a chocolate and cream livery; later they were converted to 6-wheelers when the S.M.J.R. was formed.

PRE-GROUPING PANACHE

9. *(Right)* The Northampton and Banbury Junction Railway did not have any locomotives and very little rolling stock of its own, and consequently hired them from the L.N.W.R.

Here an L.N.W.R. 0-6-0 DX goods engine hauling a rake of four L.N.W.R. coaches and an unidentified van, works away from Greens Norton Junction with a train from Brackley, and heads towards Towcester where it is due to arrive at 11.32 a.m., circa 1900.

The line for Banbury is straight ahead, while the line to Stratford-upon-Avon forks right at the junction.

10. A fine study of Great Northern locomen as they gather around the footplate of a spotless Patrick Stirling 2-2-2 7'-6" single No. 239 during Easter 1901.

G. E. R.

45924

Peterboro', G.N.

This selection of nameplates on pre-grouping locomotives that would have been seen in the county shows the different styles that were in use. 'Queen of the Belgians' and 'Marquis' were typical L.N.W.R. nameplates, made of brass, with the letters cut in and filled with a black compound. 'Coronation' was a 'one-off' with raised letters and vermilion background. *(All pictures: L. Hanson)*

11. George V No. 5000 CORONATION named to celebrate George V's Coronation and the 5000th loco to be built at Crewe — L.N.W.R.

12. Duke No. 3258 THE LIZARD, a typical Great Western nameplate with rounded ends — G.W.R.

13. Precursor No. 412 MARQUIS — L.N.W.R.

14. No. 1165 VALOUR. The Great Central memorial locomotive — G.C.R.

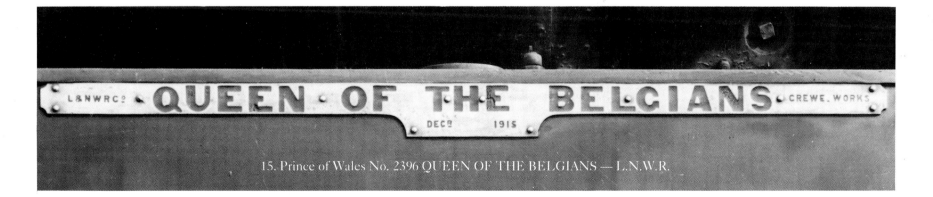

15. Prince of Wales No. 2396 QUEEN OF THE BELGIANS — L.N.W.R.

PRE-GROUPING PANACHE

16. *(Right)* Blisworth. See facing page.

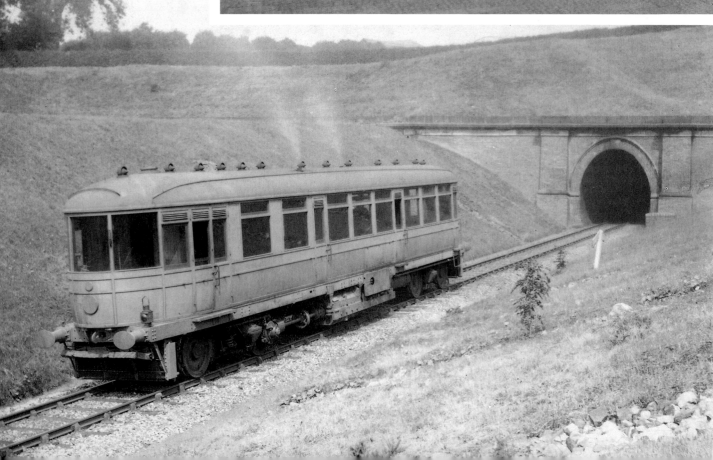

17. *(Left)* Kelmarsh Tunnel. See facing page.

L. & N. W. RY.
Thorpe

18. In 1912 the Daimler Motor Co. Ltd designed a 60-seater petrol-driven railcar for eventual trials on the L.N.W.R., but work on the project was curtailed at the outbreak of war in 1914.

In March 1918 work recommenced and tests were carried out through 1919 when these photographs were taken at Blisworth (16 — see facing page), the south end of Kelmarsh tunnel (17 — see facing page), and at Thorpe on the Peterborough to Blisworth line (above).

The trials were successful, but the L.N.W.R. lost interest, mainly because of its non-standard design, and the railcar returned to the Daimler works sidings until the middle of 1921 when the project was abandoned altogether. (*Thorpe: Samuel Freeman; others: Ron Cadman collection*)

19. Not many photographs were taken at the turn of the century of trains 'really going for it', simply because the glass plate emulsions and camera shutter speeds of that time were slow, and consequently struggled to cope with moving objects. In this fine action shot a renewed Precedent class 2-4-0 storms up the gradient towards Roade with a Euston-bound express. It is about to cross the bridge spanning the Collingtree to Milton Malsor road.

PRE-GROUPING PANACHE

20. *(Left)* This typical Midland combination of clerestoried (i.e. the roof is raised with side windows over the gangway) coaches and a Johnson Midland IP 4-4-0 No. 325 of 1877 vintage was photographed in the early 1920's. The train is seen romping past Kingsthorpe with a Northampton to Market Harborough local. *(W.J.S. Meredith)*

21. *(Below)* Renewed Precedent 2-4-0 No. 1187 CHANDOS powers a down express of six-wheelers away from the Blisworth stop circa 1900. Locomotives in this class were known as 'Jumbos' and were the mainstay of express passenger haulage at this time.

PRE-GROUPING PANACHE

22. (*Right*) Towards the end of the pre-grouping period in the early 1920's, an L.N.W.R. 'Jumbo' and 'Claughton' haul a varied assortment of stock away from Northampton Castle and over the bridge spanning the River Nene adjacent to Victoria Park with a north-bound train. (*W. Mallard*)

23. (*Left*) Through typical Northamptonshire countryside on a hot summer's day in 1900, a Johnson 4-2-2 7'-6" single No. 76 enters the south end of Glendon and Rushton station with a St Pancras to Leicester express. The combination would have looked superb with the Midland red locomotive set off by the brass safety-valve cover and matching Midland red coaches.

20. *(Left)* This typical Midland combination of clerestoried (i.e. the roof is raised with side windows over the gangway) coaches and a Johnson Midland IP 4-4-0 No. 325 of 1877 vintage was photographed in the early 1920's. The train is seen romping past Kingsthorpe with a Northampton to Market Harborough local. *(W.J.S. Meredith)*

21. *(Below)* Renewed Precedent 2-4-0 No. 1187 CHANDOS powers a down express of six-wheelers away from the Blisworth stop circa 1900. Locomotives in this class were known as 'Jumbos' and were the mainstay of express passenger haulage at this time.

PRE-GROUPING PANACHE

22. *(Right)* Towards the end of the pre-grouping period in the early 1920's, an L.N.W.R. 'Jumbo' and 'Claughton' haul a varied assortment of stock away from Northampton Castle and over the bridge spanning the River Nene adjacent to Victoria Park with a north-bound train. *(W. Mallard)*

23. *(Left)* Through typical Northamptonshire countryside on a hot summer's day in 1900, a Johnson 4-2-2 7'-6" single No. 76 enters the south end of Glendon and Rushton station with a St Pancras to Leicester express. The combination would have looked superb with the Midland red locomotive set off by the brass safety-valve cover and matching Midland red coaches.

24. The 10.15 a.m. Harwich to Birmingham 'Harwich express' powers through Wansford station at full speed during 1904/05 behind a Jubilee class compound 4-4-0 (believed to be No. 1932 ANSON) watched by signalmen J. Waters and F. Dawkes.

Northampton driver Hobbs is in charge of the Jubilee which would have worked a Northampton to Peterborough local before picking up the 'Harwich express' from a Great Eastern locomotive at Peterborough East station. *(Samuel Freeman)*

CARRYING THE PASSENGERS

25. Passenger Mabel Meredith seems to be having second thoughts about making the huge step up into the carriage standing at Northampton Castle platform 8 while awaiting the 1.37 p.m. train to Coventry on Saturday, 2 March 1929. *(W.J.S. Meredith)*

L. M. & S. R.
Northampton

26. *(Right)* A Webb 2-4-2 tank No. 6746 stands at the head of the Blisworth motor set, while Kirtley rebuilt Johnson single framed Midland 2-4-0 No. 77 stands with the Peterborough train. Both await departure to transport their passengers from Castle station's bay platforms 4 and 5 respectively on Saturday 9 September 1933.

27. *(Below)* Another view of the Blisworth motor set at platform 4 on Tuesday 5 September 1933. Webb tank No. 6723 heads the two ex-London and North Western coaches that have been freshly painted in L.M.S. maroon livery. *(Both pictures: W.J.S. Meredith)*

A part from official photographs, interior views of railway carriages were rarely photographed. The photographer here took the opportunity to record these views while coaches were in temporary store at Northampton Castle station.

28. *(Left)* Photographed on 16 March 1929 this view shows the interior of an L.M.S. open 3rd saloon No. 5943, taken from the second interior vestibule, showing the ornately patterned moquette material and polished mahogany timber, with clusters of electric lights overhead.
(W.J.S. Meredith)

29. *(Right)* This view photographed on 3 May 1930 shows a gas lit ex-Lancashire and Yorkshire vestibule coach with luggage racks situated over the seat backs. The photographer noted that the seats were particularly low in comparison with other coaches.
(W.J.S. Meredith)

30. Wheel tapper L.J. Bryant goes about his work on the coach wheels of the 'Sunny South Express' on 13 July 1929. This ex-West Coast Joint Stock clerestoried dining car, of late 1890s vintage, was built jointly by the London and North Western and Caledonian railways for use on their prestigious Anglo-Scottish expresses. It was luxuriously fitted out internally, and rode superbly on the six-wheel bogies. It is seen here on far humbler duty, painted in L.M.S. colours as No. 10469. The wheel tapper listens to the familiar ring of a sound wheel. If he gets a dull thud, then the metal tyre may be cracked. This would have meant the passengers being taken off and the carriage shunted out of the train, no matter what delay or other disruptions the action might have caused. *(W.J.S. Meredith)*

31. This interior view of an elegant gas lit Midland railway clerestoried dining car was photographed at Northampton on 1 November 1930. *(W.J.S. Meredith)*

32. A view looking down the corridor of a London and North Western coach on 11 May 1929 (L.M.S. No. 8260) showing the unusual hinged doors leading to the compartments instead of the more usual sliding type. *(W.J.S. Meredith)*

CARRYING THE PASSENGERS

33. The low winter sunshine of 4 January 1936 glints on the red boiler of Precursor 4-4-0 No. 5304 GREYHOUND as the engine leaves Northampton Castle with the 3-30 p.m. Saturdays only local to Bletchley.

Railway workers from Wolverton and Bletchley often used their privilege tickets for shopping trips to Northampton, and regularly returned home on this train. *(L. Hanson)*

34. An L.M.S. dining car forms part of the 'Sunny South Express' with the carriage nameboard attached. *(W.J.S. Meredith)*

35. *(Top of facing page)* The 'Sunny South Express' prepares for departure from platform 1 at Northampton Castle on Saturday 28 April 1928. This train was very popular with holiday makers bound for the south coast. As a direct service it avoided the inconvenience of crossing London with children and luggage to change trains.

Starting from Manchester (10.40 a.m.) and Liverpool (10.35 a.m.) the two sections joined up at Crewe, then headed south, stopping at Nuneaton, Rugby, Northampton and Willesden.

At Willesden a Southern region locomotive would take over the train and skirt the Metropolis via the West London line through Kensington to Clapham Junction, before proceeding to Brighton, Eastbourne, Bexhill and Hastings where it was due to arrive at 6.25 p.m.

Here at Northampton the 2.00 p.m. departure time is imminent as wheel tapper Jack Richards inspects the motion of well burnished crimson lake Royal Scot No. 6143 MAIL, constructed at the North British Locomotive Company works only six months previously. *(W.J.S. Meredith)*

CARRYING THE PASSENGERS

36 and 37. *(Left)* When the first batch of 50 'Royal Scots' were built for the L.M.S. in 1927, they had such a profound impact, both on the tracks and with the Press that the author S.P.B. Mais wrote in his book about the locomotives and their names:

> "When she is at rest, we have time to admire the austere beauty of her lines, the rhythm of her long crimson boiler and high glittering wheels and staunch piston rods of immense strength.

> "Racing sweetly along the polished track under full steam, she is the embodiment of power and speed, perfect symbol of the poetry of motion."

This study of No. 6146 JENNY LIND at the head of the 'Sunny South Express' on 22 March 1930 at Northampton Castle station shows the locomotive's proportions as described by S.P.B. Mais.

Jenny Lind was a famous Prima Donna, discovered singing on the streets of her native Stockholm. She made such an impact with her wonderful voice when she came to London in 1847 that a locomotive was named after her. A brass plaque below the nameplate of 6146 shows an engraving of the original Jenny Lind locomotive as built for the Midland Railway. *(Both pictures: W.J.S. Meredith)*

A cheap day excursion to the seaside used to be a very popular event, even though on a cross-country route a good deal of the day would be spent travelling to and from one's destination.

38. Here at Northampton Castle young and old alike wait in anticipation for the train to Hunstanton on Wednesday, 7 August 1963. Wymans bookstall appears to have been doing a good trade in comics, with the *Beano* much in evidence. *(Northampton Chronicle and Echo)*

CARRYING THE PASSENGERS

39. The train arrives behind Rugby-based Stanier Jubilee No. 45672 ANSON. After the scramble for seats the passengers settle down and find their own ways of passing the time while en-route to Hunstanton. *(Northampton Chronicle and Echo)*

CARRYING THE PASSENGERS

40. Having arrived at Peterborough East station with a train from Cromer, ex-L.N.E.R. B17 4-6-0 No. 61635 MILTON begins shunting manoeuvres and pulls the front coach away from the train on Thursday 9 September 1954. Passengers and photographer will have to wait patiently for their connection to Northampton. *(W.J.S. Meredith)*

41. This interesting overall view of Weedon station on Saturday 15 March 1958 shows Ivatt 2-6-2 tank No. 41285 having arrived with the 12.55 p.m. Leamington train standing in the bay platform while Black 5 No. 45203, which is not visible, waits to depart with the 12.18 p.m. Watford to Rugby local train. The Rugby train gave a good connection for passengers wishing to travel to stations en route to Leamington. It was due to leave at 2.04 p.m., while the Leamington train was booked for a 2.16 p.m. departure. (J.N. Simms)

CARRYING THE PASSENGERS

42. Northampton Bridge Street level crossing on Saturday 2 May 1964. Ivatt class 2MT No. 41227 pushes its train towards Bridge Street station with a local train from Wellingborough whilst the usual build-up of traffic is in evidence. An Austin Cambridge in excellent external condition compares strikingly with the neglected shabby condition of 41227. *(Trevor Riddle)*

43. *(Above)* A most tranquil scene at Higham Ferrers on Saturday 2 October 1954 as fireman Reg Mayes chats to a young enthusiast from the footplate of Johnson 'Linnet' 0-4-4 tank No. 58091. Presently the train will be making its short return trip to Rushden and Wellingborough. *(Ken Fairey)*

44. *(Above)* Four years later only the motive power has changed as Ivatt Class 2 No. 41328 from Wellingborough shed stands at Higham Ferrers

45. *(Below)* A notice announcing the opening of the branch line to goods and mineral traffic on 1 September 1893. *(P. Butler collection)*

MIDLAND RAILWAY

OPENING of NEW STATIONS
AT
RUSHDEN
AND
HIGHAM FERRERS.

The Midland Railway Company hereby give notice that their

NEW LINE FROM IRCHESTER TO RUSHDEN AND HIGHAM FERRERS

WILL BE OPENED FOR

GOODS & MINERAL TRAFFIC
On SEPTEMBER 1st, 1893.

EXCELLENT WAREHOUSE and **YARD ACCOMMODATION** is provided at each Station, and **Goods** and **Merchandise** will be collected and delivered by the COMPANY'S OWN TEAMS.

RATES AND OTHER INFORMATION may be obtained from the Station Master at either place; Mr. Joseph Shaw, Mineral Manager, Derby; or Mr. W. E. Adie, Goods Manager, Midland Railway, Derby.

GEO. H. TURNER, General Manager.

Derby, August, 1893.

Bemrose & Sons, Limited, Printers, London and Derby.

station having arrived with an afternoon local train from Wellingborough during the summer of 1958. *(Tony Heighton)*

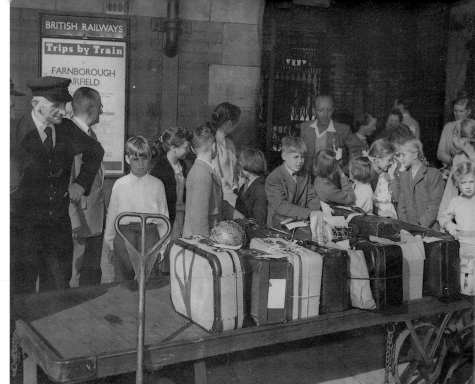

47. *(Above)* At the height of a late 1950s summer, a group of European school children arrive at Kettering station for their holidays, seen here placing luggage on to the trolley under the watchful eye of porter Joe Gates. The billboard advertises trips to the forthcoming Farnborough Air Show in September. *(Evening Telegraph, N.B. Scott collection)*

46. *(Left)* In the grip of the severe winter of 1962/63 a Fowler 2-6-4 Tank No. 42355 makes a vigorous departure from Kettering station with a local train to Leicester during February 1963. Smoke and steam swirl around the platforms in the icy cold conditions with the warmest place to be found on the footplate, where for once the footplate crew are enjoying the warmth of the fire. *(Trevor Riddle)*

CARRYING THE PASSENGERS

48. (Left) At Northampton St John's Street station a Midland 'Linnet' 0-4-4 tank No. 1260 replenishes its water tanks on Friday 24 March 1939 before its departure with a local branch line train to Bedford. The engine is still in its original condition with a brass safety valve cover and the 15D shed plate on its smokebox door indicates its home shed of Bedford.

St John's Street station closed on 3 July 1939, and passengers for Bedford and Wellingborough then had to leave from Northampton Castle or Bridge Street stations. (W.J.S. Meredith)

49. (Right) A March 1939 view of St John's Street showing the unique structure of this Midland station with its bonded warehouses in the vaults below. Behind the station is the carriage shed where the lines terminated.

The row of terraced houses front onto Victoria Gardens with the nearest arch giving access through to Guildhall Road. (W.J.S. Meredith)

At the north end of Wellingborough Midland Road station the signalbox stood dominant for over 95 years. Whilst train-spotting on the platform it was a joy to listen to the distinctive signal bells ringing to announce the approach of a train. Then the sound of the semaphore signals being raised would fill one with anticipation of what engine would arrive on the next train.

50. (Right) An unidentified class 9F stands in the siding in readiness to haul a local stopping train to Leicester; not normally a duty for which it would be rostered. (L.W. Roy)

51. (Below) A standard 2MT tank No. 84007 from Wellingborough shed brings a train into platform 5 to form the Higham Ferrers local during 1959. (Tony Heighton)

52. The last day of through passenger services on the Great Central Railway as Black 5 No. 44872 draws into Brackley station with a semi-fast train to London Marylebone from Nottingham on the morning of 3 September 1966. Some six years earlier the real express trains on the Great Central had ended, to be replaced by an inferior service as far as the long distance traveller was concerned. There were only three daytime semi-fast trains each way during the day at this time, and with no refreshment facilities available the trains would only have appealed to short distance travellers such as shoppers and commuters! The complete journey in fact took over three hours. (Norman Parker)

CARRYING THE PASSENGERS

53. Standing on the platforms at Rugby Midland station passengers could not fail to be impressed by the grandeur of the place, especially the splendid roof covering the station. Resembling more a large terminal city station it was a grand place to see the trains come and go. The crescendo of sounds filled the air and echoed around the platforms, with smoke and steam remaining well in evidence after the passing of trains. On this occasion a northbound football excursion from London to Birmingham hauled by Britannia class No. 70021 MORNING STAR eases past Rugby No. 2 signalbox under the watchful eye of an elderly gentleman on Saturday 31 March 1962. This was one of three Britannia-hauled specials in connection with an FA Cup semi-final football match at Villa Park between Fulham and Burnley. *(J.N. Simms)*

CARRYING THE PASSENGERS

54. Passenger movements at Rugby were many with the comings and goings of expresses as well as all the local traffic.

In this early 1951 view, Fowler Patriot No. 45543 HOME GUARD and Stanier Coronation Pacific No. 46252 CITY OF LEICESTER provide ample power to restart a northbound express away from platform 1, while the signalman in No. 4 box observes proceedings from a grandstand viewpoint.

'City of Leicester' appears to be painted in B.R. lined blue livery, and both locomotives carry the words 'British Railways' on their tenders, a style soon to be superseded by the 'Lion and Wheel' emblem.
(John G. Click — National Railway Museum)

55. A typical station scene at Kettering in the mid-1950s as holiday makers chat amongst themselves seemingly oblivious of their train drawing into platform 5. *(Northamptonshire Advertiser — N.B. Scott collection)*

CARRYING THE PASSENGERS

56. A busy scene on platform No. 1 at Kettering station with the ever-present station trolleys littering the foreground while passengers join the local train to Northampton on Saturday 2 May 1964. The footplate crew on Ivatt class 2MT No. 41225 share a conversation with their colleagues, no doubt reflecting the fact that this was to be the last weekend of passenger services to Northampton. *(Trevor Riddle)*

57. Having deposited its passengers, the 10.22 a.m. train from Northampton pulls out of Wellingborough Midland Road station to clear the main line. The train is in the capable hands of Ivatt 2-6-2 tank No. 41218 on a cold March day in 1964. The mid-morning stopping train to St Pancras, in the form of a diesel multiple unit, awaits departure from platform 2. (L.H. Cummings)

CARRYING THE PASSENGERS

58. It appears as though driver, fireman and Midland 0-4-4 tank No. 58085 are having an easy day's work on the Higham Ferrers branch during Saturday 5 April 1952. A push and pull train with only one coach was a rare sight on the branch. In this fine portrait the 11.18 a.m. from Higham Ferrers has just arrived after being pushed to Wellingborough Midland Road station. *(Ian L. Wright)*

59. Freezing fog and snow were causing problems for both passengers and photographer at Northampton Castle on Saturday 31 December 1927.

The train from Euston to Crewe was due out at 1.37 p.m. but did not arrive until 2.18 p.m. behind one of Bowen-Cooke's Claughton 4-6-0s No. 5968 JOHN O'GROAT and beautifully groomed Royal Scot No. 6125 LANCASHIRE WITCH.

Conditions were grim, and a time exposure was necessary to capture the image even at 2.25 in the afternoon.

The train soon departed, and the crisp exhaust beats of the two powerful locomotives reverberated through the air as they made a determined effort to 'get away' and make up some of the time already lost. (W.J.S. Meredith)

CARRYING THE PASSENGERS

60. Shrouded in steam, 3F No. 43568 makes a vigorous start from Blisworth S.M.J. signalbox after her crew had picked up the single line staff from the signalman. The 3F is hauling the very last 6.50 p.m. passenger train from Blisworth to Stratford-upon-Avon as dusk falls on Saturday 5 April 1952, the last day of passenger services, an event commemorated by the use of a Union Jack tied to the front of the locomotive. *(Norman Parker)*

61. and 62. Various experiments were carried out during the 1930s with different types of railcar. The first on the L.M.S. was the 'Armstrong Shell Express' which was built by Armstrong-Whitworth and ran on diesoleum oil. It was very similar in appearance to the one illustrated here standing in bay platform 4 at Northampton Castle in the 1930s. The car was built by Armstrong-Whitworth and, according to the photographer's notes, was a 'D2L coach'. *(Both pictures: W.J.S. Meredith)*

63. and 64. This is the experimental Coventry Pneumatic Railcar No. 2 in bay platform 3 at Northampton Castle in 1937. The vehicle was 54' long with an aluminium body, and had seating capacity for 56 passengers.

The driver sat in the raised cockpit which gave vision either way and avoided having to turn the railcar. The luggage compartment behind the roller shutters had capacity for 15 cwt of luggage or other goods.

The cars were petrol driven and the engine compartment was vented by the openable rear flaps when in motion, and by the roof flap when stationary (as shown in the illustrations).

Two of the cars were built and ran extensive trials in the Northampton, Oxford and Rugby areas of the L.M.S., but the company declined the offer of taking them into stock, and they were eventually broken up. *(Both pictures: W.J.S. Meredith)*

Various means of motive power were tried out on branch lines in an endeavour to cut costs and keep them open. Unfortunately within the county this didn't help, and the inevitable closure of lines followed.

65. *(Above)* One of the Park Royal four wheel rail buses No. M79973 stops at Piddington en-route to Bedford on Saturday 8 August 1959. It makes one wonder if any passengers used this station apart from the odd rambler or photographer. These rail buses were not popular with passengers, the car's short wheelbase resulted in considerable 'bouncing' at the front and rear, giving a very uncomfortable ride. They were later transferred to Scotland and worked branch lines around Ayr. *(J. Spencer Gilks)*

66. *(Right)* A two car diesel multiple unit glides into Olney station on a damp and dreary Saturday 19 November 1960. The passengers will welcome the warmth of the carriage for their trip to Northampton. *(J. Spencer Gilks)*

CARRYING THE PASSENGERS

67. In the mid-1950s Derby works constructed two motor brake second railcars for use on the Banbury, Buckingham, Bletchley service, which they worked until closure of the branch at the end of 1960. On a very pleasant day in June 1959 passengers mount the platform steps to board one of the railcars at Brackley L.N.W.R. station for the service to Buckingham and Bletchley — once a common branch line occurrence around the county and sadly no longer a part of the railway scene. (*L.H. Cummings*)

Within the image:

NO SMOKING

1X68

HALF-DAY EXCURSION

Returns from:

Peterboro East   at 5.30 p.m.

FOR

Wellingboro' L.Rd.,
Castle Ashby,
Northampton B.st.

and

68. Driver Walter Marriott and Fireman Rodney Pearson were the footplate crew on Class 5 No. 45302 that worked the football excursion to Peterborough on Saturday 11 May 1963. So many supporters turned up to travel to the game that two more coaches were added to the 10-coach train. The Cobblers needed to win to become Division III champions, and sure enough a 4-2 victory resulted in a happy return journey. When the firemen's friends travelling in the first coach started looking out of the windows pulling faces at their colleague on the footplate, an application of water from a hose soon made them get back into their seats! It was all part of the day's entertainment. *(Northampton Chronicle and Echo)*

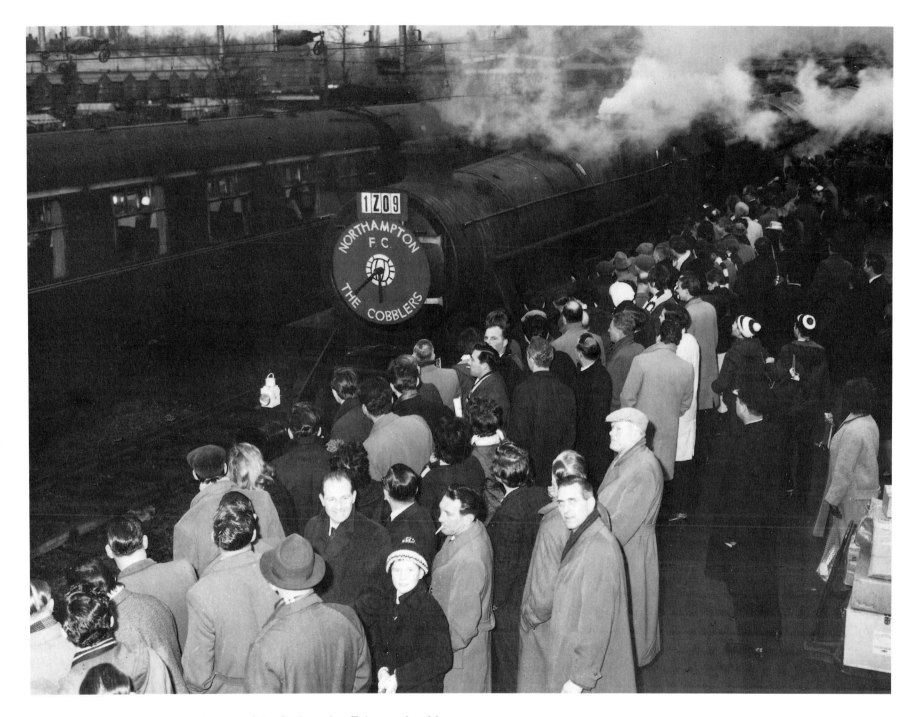

69. Excitement mounts at the thought of the forthcoming F.A. cup tie with Chelsea as Cobblers supporters crowd platform 1 at Northampton Castle station on Saturday 9 January 1965. The special headboard adorns Northampton Black 5 No. 45398 as the train pulls in for the trip to Euston. *(Northampton Chronicle and Echo)*

CARRYING THE PASSENGERS

70. On the return trip from Chelsea it's all been too much for these young ladies, even their transistor radio cannot keep them awake. *(Northampton Chronicle and Echo)*

71. These youngsters seem determined not to let the 4-1 defeat at Chelsea get them down as they play games while making the most of their journey home to Northampton. *(Northampton Chronicle and Echo)*

CARRYING THE PASSENGERS

Railway clubs and societies frequently organized rail tours for their members, usually at a weekend, and they would traverse lines and branches that were either due to shut or had already been shut to passenger traffic.

72. On Saturday 22 September 1962 the South Bedfordshire Locomotive Club organized a rail tour called 'The Banburian' and obtained ex-L.N.W.R. 7F 0-8-0 No. 48930 from Bescot shed to work the special.

Starting from Luton Bute Street, it ran to Leighton Buzzard, along the West Coast main line to Bletchley where it took the cross-country route to Verney Junction, Buckingham, Brackley and Banbury Merton Street. (Buckingham to Banbury passenger services were withdrawn at the end of 1960.) Here the train has arrived at Banbury Merton Street, and enthusiasts admire the old 'Super D' which is fitted with a tender cab.

These freight locomotives were always in a filthy state while in normal service, so obviously 48930 has been spruced up for the occasion. Unfortunately the old lady was withdrawn and scrapped three months later. (Robin Puryer)

73. Northampton Castle plays host to a Stephenson Locomotive Society special on Saturday 14 April 1962. Originating from Birmingham, the 240 mile round trip via Northampton, Bedford, Hitchin, Hertford North, Welwyn Garden City, Hatfield, Luton, Dunstable, Leighton Buzzard, Weedon and Leamington Spa cost just 32/6d. The train having arrived at Northampton behind one of the last surviving Fowler 2P 4-4-0s No. 40646 becomes the centre of attraction as much clicking of shutters is performed by the travelling enthusiasts. Fowler 2-6-2 tank No. 40026 is seen standing on the centre road and was later piloted by 40646 for the trip to Bedford. 40026 was shedded at Kentish Town and fitted with condensing apparatus for working London suburban services. (Robin Puryer)

OUT ON THE
TRACKS

74. Fighting for adhesion on the damp rails, Stanier Jubilee No. 45741 LEINSTER blasts smoke and steam high into the air in its effort to get the heavily loaded 9.45 a.m. Wolverhampton to Euston train away from Northampton Castle on Sunday 10 February 1952. Making for Euston via Blisworth, the footplate men will be glad to clear the smoke-logged void under West Bridge. (Ross Smith)

75. In the days when the length of trains seemed never ending, the Sunday diverted 'Royal Scot' eases past Northampton No. 1 signalbox on its way north as rain clouds gather overhead during 12 August 1951. Hauling the train is Coronation Pacific No. 46227 DUCHESS OF DEVONSHIRE still retaining the sloping smokebox top from being previously streamlined. Until the coming of the diesels one would have expected to see nothing less than a 'Duchess on the Scot'. *(L. Hanson)*

76. *(Left)* With the sun glinting on her boiler and seemingly floating on a bed of steam from the sanders, Stanier Jubilee No. 45688 POLYPHEMUS provides a highly evocative image as she gets away from the south end of Rugby with a Wolverhampton to London two-hour express in the early 1950s. *(John G. Click/National Railway Museum)*

OUT ON THE TRACKS

77. *(Left)* A keen wind whips away the smoke and steam from Ivatt 2-6-2 tank No. 41218 as the engine pulls out of platform 4 at Northampton Castle with the 10.22 a.m. train to Wellingborough on a cold March day in 1964. In the distance a Stanier 8F has steam to spare while on shunting duties at the carriage sheds. *(L.H. Cummings)*

78. *(Right)* Steam rebounds from the soffit of West Bridge as Thompson B1 4-6-0 No. 61204 emerges into the sunlight from platform 1 at Northampton Castle with a Peterborough-bound local passenger during February 1962. When Peterborough Spital Bridge shed closed in 1960 the motive power for these trains was provided by March loco shed, coded 31B, until services were withdrawn on 2 May 1964. *(L.H. Cummings)*

79. This is indeed a rare photograph, taken from the footplate of a Stanier Coronation Streamlined Pacific on a northbound express, which is about to pass a sister engine heading an express bound for Euston, at Milton crossing between Roade and Blisworth circa 1938.

Unfortunately neither locomotive can be identified, but with the vibration, speed and excitement of the occasion it's a wonder the photographer managed to take a picture at all.

What a spectacle it would be if one of the two preserved ex-streamlined locomotives was to be re-streamlined and turned out on present day main line specials. *(Derek Lea Collection)*

80. *(Right)* A fireman's view photographed from the cab of a rebuilt Royal Scot No. 46170 BRITISH LEGION, heading an up express on the rising gradient to Kilsby Tunnel south of Rugby during the early 1950s. 'British Legion' is about to pass Hillmorton signalbox and would soon be thundering over the county boundary into Northamptonshire. *(John G. Crick/ National Railway Museum)*

81. *(Far right)* With Woodford driver Tom Pavey at the controls, Stanier Black 5 No. 44941 approaches Culworth Junction at speed on Friday 15 July 1966 with the 8.15 a.m. Nottingham to London Marylebone. Although not noticeable at first, Culworth Junction signalbox was situated on a high embankment in the middle of nowhere, and the only company for the signalman would have been the various trains that past. The line leading off to the right joined the Great Central to the Great Western at Banbury. *(Ian Lyman)*

82. Although not perfect technically, this photograph really captures the spirit of the steam age during the early 1930s. At a rain-soaked Wolverton station on Monday 1 August 1932 a brand new 'Baby Scot' No. 5987, her crimson lake boiler glistening wet, hurtles through the station with her up express on this very fast stretch of West Coast main line. The locomotive was renumbered 5504 in 1934 and named ROYAL SIGNALS in 1937. It was to see many more years service before being withdrawn and disposed of at Crewe works during March 1962. *(W.J.S. Meredith)*

L. & N. W. RY.
Wolverton

OUT ON THE TRACKS

83. Panned photographs of railway engines at speed create a powerful visual image, and examples from the 1930s are quite rare. It was especially pleasing, therefore, to find this superb action shot of Princess Royal Pacific No. 6205 PRINCESS VICTORIA passing Gayton Loops at high speed with the down 'Royal Scot' on Wednesday 18 September 1935. The massive proportions of 'Princess Victoria' can be seen in comparison to the size of her driver. Small he may be, but all that power is his to control. (W.J.S. Meredith)

84. Train photography at Roade station in the 1930s was frowned upon, and on this occasion the photographer was challenged by the Station Master as to what he was doing on the platforms. Fortunately, after some discussion, the photographer was allowed to take just two photographs before having to leave. This is one of those photographs, showing a classic study of one of Bowen-Cooke's Claughton class 4-6-0s No. 6003 hauling a section of the 'Sunny South Express' on the up slow line from Northampton on Sunday 12 March 1932. As the regulator is opened, steam from her exhaust shows up clearly in the chilly atmosphere, while the sun highlights the superb condition of her paintwork. Like the Claughton, the station, oil lamps and the houses on the right have now all passed into history. (L. Hanson)

OUT ON THE TRACKS

85. The 4.50 p.m. train from Marylebone to Bradford was named 'The South Yorkshireman', and it is seen here heading towards Leicester from Rugby Central in the capable hands of Thompson B1 No. 61164 on a summer's evening in the early 1950s. One wonders if any railway enthusiasts lived in the terraced houses on this side of Winfield Street; and with all the smoke and soot how did people dry and air their washing without it being covered in black smuts? *(John G. Click/National Railway Museum)*

86. Under the Great Central girder bridge at Rugby in the early 1950s a Standard Light Pacific No. 72005 CLAN MACGREGOR remarshalls a Glasgow to London express parcels train in readiness for the remainder of the journey southwards. Built mainly for use north of Carlisle, the 'Clans' were a very rare sight this far south of the border, and 'Clan Macgregor' was probably on a running in turn from Crewe Locomotive Works. *(John G. Click/National Railway Museum)*

OUT ON THE TRACKS

87. Early morning winter light dramatically illuminates Jubilee class No. 45703 THUNDERER as the engine sets off to London, Euston, with a passenger train in the early 1950s. In the background the eerie structure of the bridge carrying the Great Central railway stands out boldly. John Click, the photographer, enjoyed taking photographs of trains 'going away', and this one is particularly striking, showing the amount of thought that has gone into choosing the time and the place for the picture. *(John G. Click/National Railway Museum)*

88. *(Left)* In the far southwestern part of Northamptonshire the Great Western Railway runs through the county from just south of Aynho station to within a mile of Banbury station, a total of some five miles. Along this stretch of track water troughs used to be located during the steam days from Aynho Junction to near Kings Sutton station. King class No. 6020 KING HENRY IV rushes past over the troughs with one of the hourly Birmingham to London, Paddington, services at lunchtime on Saturday 23 June 1962. Many of the King class locomotives were withdrawn during 1962 and by the middle of July 1962 6020 had also joined these ranks. *(J.N. Simms)*

89. *(Left, on facing page)* Castle class No. 5026 CRICCIETH CASTLE heads towards its home shed of Wolverhampton (Stafford Road) with the 'Cambrian Coast Express' from Paddington to Aberystwyth. The train is seen on Saturday, 8 September 1962, approaching King's Sutton station, one of only three stations on the Great Western Railway in Northamptonshire. The other two, of course, were Aynho and Aynho Park, both of which have since closed. *(Robin Puryer)*

90. *(Above)* Stanier Jubilee class No. 45594 BHOPAL swings round the curve on the approach to Kettering South signalbox with the southbound 'Thames-Clyde Express' during the summer of 1957. Headlands Bridge, which overlooks the railway at this point, was a favourite viewing spot for many local trainspotters and enthusiasts. The 'Thames-Clyde Express' would normally pass early evening, so was eagerly awaited. *(Tony Heighton)*

OUT ON THE TRACKS

Despite the fact that steam-hauled trains ran in all kinds of weather conditions, photographers in general lacked the enthusiasm to brave the elements in order to obtain photographs in adverse conditions. Of course, many of them would never press the camera shutter unless the sun shone, and with steam trains an everday occurrence, it was just a matter of waiting for a sunny day before taking out the camera. Fortunately, some photographers did go out in inclement conditions, and the two pictures on this spread, and others throughout the book, show just how dramatic the results could be.

91. The rain is really lashing down from a leaden sky at Roade cutting on this miserable summer's day in 1957. On the down main, Coronation Pacific No. 46253 CITY OF ST ALBANS powers her Anglo/Scottish express out of the cutting and under the high arches of 'Black Bridge'. The beats of her exhaust are almost visible in the layers of smoke emanating from the double chimney as the driver gives 'City of St Albans' her head. (C. Lucas)

92. In blizzard conditions Coronation Pacific No. 46254 CITY OF STOKE-ON-TRENT makes its way through the arctic landscape of Kingsthorpe with the Sunday's only 7.45 a.m. Blackpool to Euston train on 31 December 1961. Fortunately for the footplate men, the enclosed cab on 46254 would keep them quite well protected and warm in this hostile environment. *(Robin Puryer)*

93. One very rarely saw a Fowler Patriot leaking steam, and No. 45513 was no exception, seen here heading a down excursion from Lancashire during August 1960. Feathering steam from the safety valves indicates the boiler has reached its maximum allowable pressure and so gives the fireman a rest from firing, and allows him time to survey the surroundings as the train enters Roade station on the slow line from Northampton. *(L.W. Roy)*

OUT ON THE TRACKS

94. Bushbury-based Stanier Jubilee No. 45703 THUN-DERER makes a truly volcanic departure from Rugby as she emerges from below the Northampton line flyover in a cloud of steam and smoke while hauling a Wolverhampton to Euston two-hour express during the mid-1950s. For all 'Thunderer's' effort she receives not a second glance from the platelayers in the adjacent permanent way cabin. *(John G. Click/ National Railway Museum)*

95. Known locally as the 'Banbury Motor' the local train from Woodford Halse to Banbury makes a particularly smoky departure from Woodford behind Fairburn class 4 tank No. 42082 on Saturday 9 May 1964. Being a Saturday, the train would have been used by many shoppers travelling to Banbury, and the well-filled seats confirm this on this occasion. The locomotive was based at Woodford shed and was one of the last to leave Woodford when the shed closed a year later in June 1965. *(George Smith)*

OUT ON THE TRACKS

96. On Thursday 29 November 1949 a vintage class C12 Atlantic tank No. 7368 makes a most vigorous departure from Stamford East with an afternoon working to Essendine. It is hauling the usual branch line train for that time, made up of two non-corridor coaches and a four-wheel van.

The ex-Great Northern C12 tanks were shedded at Peterborough New England and worked a staggered fortnightly turn of duty on the Essendine branch, being sub-shedded at Stamford for the purpose. At any given time two members of the class were kept in the single road engine shed at Stamford for working the passenger and freight services, with one of the C12s returning to Peterborough each Saturday, supposedly for a boiler wash out, although this chore often had to be carried out when the engine returned to Stamford at a later date.

This evocative study was Philip Wells's first photograph to be published way back in the March 1950 issue of *Trains Illustrated*. (P.H. Wells)

97. Whitsun Bank Holiday Monday 25 May 1931 at Finedon Road witnesses Deeley Compound 4-4-0 No. 1104 powering southwards with a holiday excursion hauling no less than 13 coaches behind her tender. This was way over normal loading for an engine of this size, but with steam drifting from the safety valves, 1104 is obviously coping admirably. The lines veering off to the left gave access to Wellingborough Iron Works (illustrated in photograph 229). *(L. Hanson)*

OUT ON THE TRACKS

98. Filthy Stanier Jubilee No. 45576 BOMBAY produces incredibly black smoke on this very hot summer's evening during 1959 at Finedon station. As she thrashes past with a Sheffield bound express there are no discernible beats to her exhaust, just one continual roar which gradually fades as the train disappears towards Kettering leaving behind a long tail of exhaust. (Tony Heighton)

99. During the last weeks of the through passenger services on the Great Central Railway many photographs were taken of the final trains. In the Rugby area a popular train to photograph was the 5.15 p.m. Nottingham Victoria to Marylebone semi-fast which could be conveniently seen on the way home from work. In this dramatic illustration taken from inside the well-known 'birdcage' girder bridge at Rugby, Black 5 No. 45222 rushes its way to London on the superb summer's evening of Thursday 25 August 1966. *(J.N. Simms)*

OUT ON THE TRACKS

100. York-based V2 class No. 60847 ST PETER'S SCHOOL YORK A.D. 627 storms out of Catesby Tunnel with a train full of Leicester City football supporters heading for Wembley on Saturday 6 May 1961. This particular V2 was one of only eight to be named, and naming took place at York station on 3 April 1939 whilst the locomotive was still in L.N.E.R. ownership. *(L.W. Roy)*

101. *(Left)* Northbound trains were particularly difficult to photograph at Banbury Lane crossing as there was so little room to safely stand by the lineside. The steam trains used to come through at great speed, and if a view of the signalbox, as well as the train, was required, a head-on photograph was the only way. Patriot class No. 45519 LADY GODIVA approaches the crossing with the signalbox about to be smothered with smoke circa 1949. *(Robin Freestone)*

102. *(Right)* This view from Banbury Lane signalbox on Saturday 3 August 1957 shows Princess Royal class No. 46207 PRINCESS ARTHUR OF CONNAUGHT approaching at speed with 'The Shamrock' from Liverpool to London. The non-stop express was so-called as it provided the connection with the night steamers from Dublin and Belfast to Liverpool. The train would have left Liverpool about 8.10 a.m. and was due into Euston at 12 noon. *(P.I. Rawlinson)*

103. Out for a Sunday afternoon car ride near Long Buckby on 25 June 1961 the photographer parked his 1938 Hillman Minx and settled down on the lineside embankment situated on the Northampton loop, and waited to photograph whatever trains passed by. After a short time the familiar sounds of an approaching train were heard, and bursting from under the roadbridge came Stanier Coronation Pacific No. 46229 DUCHESS OF HAMILTON hauling a down Euston to Liverpool express. The short burst of steam from the steam-operated coal pusher in the tender, combined with the black smoke emanating from the chimney are sure signs that the fireman has been very busy 'filling the box' in readiness for when the main line is regained north of Rugby. This is a fine example of the classic traditional railway photograph, where the subject has been photographed with a large format camera from a front three-quarter view in full sunlight. (L. Hanson)

Built as part of the 1955 Modernization Plan to replace steam locomotives, English Electric Type 4 diesels became very familiar in the county during the 1960s. To many steam enthusiasts they were frowned upon and hardly ever photographed. However, some did photograph them, and these three illustrations show the diesels working at familiar landmarks in the Northampton area.

104. Although this scene may have been noticed many times by the occasional pedestrian walking along the canal towpath by the side of the locomotive shed at Northampton, photographs of the combination of train and barge are very rare. However, on this occasion George Smith, who worked on the railway at this time, had the good fortune to have his camera ready at the vital moment when the two modes of transport passed each other. D222 LACONIA slowly works its express into Northampton, after being diverted at Blisworth on Sunday 11 October 1964. Every so often a railway photographer has a bit of luck, and on this occasion that luck has helped to produce a unique picture. *(George Smith)*

OUT ON THE TRACKS

105. D372 hurtles past Banbury Lane crossing with an express for London as traffic waits to proceed to Fosters Booth. This 1965 view has been photographed from the hump bridge under which the Grand Union Canal flows. Already modernization has taken place with the replacement of the old manual gates by automatic barriers. Nowadays the crossing is still very much in use, but alas the signalbox has gone and consequently the queues of traffic have increased owing to the longer waiting gaps for trains to pass. *(George Smith)*

106. Springtime at Rothersthorpe Road crossing with just the one car waiting at the gates as D338 works north with a Scottish-bound express diverted off the main line on Sunday 11 April 1965. *(George Smith)*

MOVING THE FREIGHT

107. The clock on platform 2 at Rugby Midland station on Saturday 23 May 1964 states it is 11.50 a.m., and with time on his hands one of the footplate crew relaxes with a cup of tea. His locomotive 4F class 0-6-0 No. 44501 in extremely poor external condition is from Coalville shed and was built in 1927 in Glasgow. The train, a one-coach parcels train, originated from Leicester. Station staff are busily engaged in unloading the contents of the coach. With electrification imminent, the days of steam are numbered, and no doubt some of the workers will be glad of that, while others will miss the age of the steam engine. *(J. N. Simms)*

108. Typical S.M.J. tranquillity at Towcester station as a branch freight basks in the April sunlight of 1960 headed by Fowler 4F No. 44239 from Northampton shed. In the distance a Stanier 8F restarts a through freight from the signal on the line from Blisworth and will pass through the station to the right of the signalbox. Driver Mickey Tilling and fireman Teddy Tonks survey proceedings with interest. *(L.H. Cummings)*

109. *(Above)* Northampton-based ex-L.N.W.R. 'Cauliflower' class 2F No. 8618 moves at a leisurely pace past Ashton on the up slow on Saturday afternoon 26 May 1934. The cattle wagons would have transported livestock to Northampton in readiness for the Saturday cattle market, and 8618 is seen returning empty wagons southwards. The Cauliflowers were a long-lived class being built around the turn of the century, and nearly 70 survived into nationalization in 1948 with the last member of the class not being withdrawn until 1955. *(L. Hanson)*

110. *(Right)* This is a rather unusual working for a Webb passenger tank as No. 6694 is seen moving through Northampton Castle in the mid-1930s with an evening inter-yard freight from 'Cotton Yards' to 'Down Sidings'. *(W.J.S. Meredith)*

MOVING THE FREIGHT

111. *(Right)* One of the Fowler class 7F 0-8-0, known as 'Austin Sevens', No. 9501 'opens up' through the centre road at Northampton Castle with a Toton to Brentwood sidings coal train on 4 July 1931. This train, due through the station around 3.25 p.m., was often a sight worth watching as the drivers worked the trains up to speed for a run at the 1 in 200 bank towards Roade. This was only achievable providing the guard kept the guards van brake screwed down to keep the train's couplings taut and prevent them closing up, otherwise when the locomotive started to accelerate on the gradient a snatch would occur which could break the train in half. Consequently, the sight and sound of the train clattering through the centre road at substantial speed with sparks shooting out from the braked wheels of the guards van was at times quite spectacular.
(W.J.S. Meredith)

112. A view into the cab of ex-L.N.W.R. 'Super D' No. 49432 finds the driver about to restart his freight train from the signal gantry just south of Spencer bridge Northampton on 17 September 1960. The 'Super D' was being assisted on this occasion by Stanier 8F No. 48012. *(L.W. Roy)*

113. An ex-L.N.W.R. 'Super D' No. 49310 works the 'Wolverton's' bunker first through Roade whilst returning to Northampton during September 1960. On this round trip the locomotive shunted the station yards at Roade and Castlethorpe before proceeding to Wolverton Works where it shunted the sidings. *(L.H. Cummings)*

114. *(Above)* A superb study of class WD 2-8-0 'Austerity' No. 90161, from Colwick shed, clanking past Northampton No. 2 signalbox with a coal train from the Midlands, and heading south on a clear sunny afternoon in March 1960. The impressive collection of semaphore signals, from the end of the platform to Spencer Bridge in the backgound, will long be remembered by local enthusiasts. The 'Dub-dees', as they were affectionately called, although not popular with enthusiasts did much sterling work hauling freight trains around the county. *(L.W. Roy)*

115. and 116. *(Facing page)* Freshly out of the works Toton-based class 8F 2-8-0 No. 48194 brings an empty coal train past the signal gantry near Northampton No. 4 signalbox, while another 8F waits for the 'right away' with a full coal train for the south. 48194 then sets off in the direction of Market Harborough on its way back to the Nottinghamshire coalfield on Saturday 7 October 1961. In the background the district around Kingsthorpe Hollow is well in evidence, including, in the top left corner, Barrett's shoe factory. Owing to the liability of flooding, the land in this area of Northampton has always remained quite rural. *(Both pictures: L.W. Roy)*

MOVING THE FREIGHT

117. This must be one of the finest action pictures of a Beyer-Garratt 2-6-0:0-6-2 ever photographed in the county. The wintry setting is on the northern edge of Northamptonshire on the approach to Stamford station with Easton Hillside in the background, and the frozen waters of the River Welland on the right. No. 47969 makes an impressive sight as it strides away from a signal check with a coal train from the Midlands to Peterborough on Friday 4 January 1952.
(P.H. Wells)

118. Beyer-Garratt 2-6-0:0-6-2 No. 47972 makes an impressive sight as it thrashes south near Great Bowden on the approach to Market Harborough on Saturday 16 February 1957. The Northamptonshire boundary is less than two miles away, and the driver will know when he has reached it as the long five-mile climb up to Desborough begins at that point. The Garratts will be fondly remembered for the sight and sound they produced hauling their long freight trains along the Midland main line. *(R. Gammage)*

MOVING THE FREIGHT

Moving the Freight

119. *(Facing page)* With the fireman relaxing in his seat on the footplate soaking up the sunshine on a gorgeous summer's day rebuilt Royal Scot class No. 46139 THE WELCH REGIMENT eases her long up mixed freight round the long curve from Wellingborough Midland Road station and past the sidings of the Morris Motors factory on Thursday 8 June 1961. The locomotive is heading back to its home shed at Kentish Town and, unusually, is hauling a parcels van amongst its many freight wagons. *(Ken Fairey)*

120. *(Above)* A hot summer's day down by the railway at Wellingborough produces a superb sight of a pair of Riddles 9Fs No. 92094 and 92153 working a train of fitted coal wagons on a test run between Brent and Toton on Sunday 15 June 1958. With Mill Lane Bridge in the background and the lodging house for railwaymen on the left, the train eases past after passing through Wellingborough Midland Road station. In the cab of 92094 a glimpse of the locomotive inspector with his bowler hat looking out at the photographer can be seen. *(Ken Fairey)*

121. and 122. The infamous Kettering Ivatt class 2-6-0 No. 43048 eases its freight train past Kettering South signalbox on the approach to Headlands Road Bridge on Thursday 9 November 1961. Almost two years earlier 43048, whilst hauling a local passenger train, collided with wagons from a derailed freight train north of Kettering station. In the smaller illustration 43048 lies rather forlorn on its side on Monday 18 January 1960 after the accident. *(Main photograph: Ken Fairey — small photograph: Chronicle and Echo)*

MOVING THE FREIGHT

123. and 124. Kettering Iron & Coal Co's sidings signalbox was located some one and half miles north of Kettering station on the Midland main line. From the footbridge just north of the box an excellent view of trains working on the main line, as well as the shunting in the adjacent Kettering Furnaces, could be enjoyed. On Saturday 22 March 1958 an 8F class No. 48390 climbs hard up the 1 in 160 gradient towards Glendon South Junction and then towards Corby and Manton with a train of iron ore for the Midlands. Meanwhile Ivatt 'Mogul' No. 46404, based at Kettering shed, arrives with empty wagons for the sidings. One of the industrial shunting engines can be seen at work in the sidings. Although the Kettering Furnaces closed a year later, iron ore continued to be sent to Corby steelworks until October 1962, and it was another five years before the signalbox closed on 10 September 1967. *(Both pictures: R. Gammage)*

125. A lone gas lamp in the foreground makes a vain attempt to cheer up a miserable day as one of the Franco Crosti-boilered Standard 2-10-0s No. 92028, still in its original form, powers a down fitted freight past Bedford locomotive shed on Thursday 4 September 1958. The ex-Lancashire and Yorkshire class 2P tank No. 50646 stands in store at the shed yard and would be taken away for scrap two months later. *(Ken Fairey)*

MOVING THE FREIGHT

126. The Stanier 8Fs were probably the most successful class of freight locomotive ever built, being constructed by all four British Railway companies during the 1940s. Including those built for War Department use overseas, a total of 852 were constructed between 1935 and 1946. Here we see the pioneer of the class, No. 48000 from Nottingham, working purposefully through Wellingborough on the up slow line during Sunday 25 April 1959. (R. Gammage)

127. The photographer has braved the intense cold and wintry conditions to venture up to Rothersthorpe Road bridge to witness the passing of yet another coal train slogging its way out of Northampton and south towards London on Sunday 27 January 1963. Class 8F 2-8-0 No. 48077 of Nuneaton shed is the locomotive at the head of the train, and no doubt was used on other Sunday coal trains in an attempt to clear backlogs of traffic due to the severe weather conditions during this period. Operational difficulties were widespread at this time caused by the extremely hard winter weather, and one of the main problems was that of water columns freezing up. (G.R. Onley)

MOVING THE FREIGHT

128. A coal train staggers out of Northampton Castle station past the Corporation's West Bridge Depot and up the 1 in 200 bank towards Hunsbury Hill tunnel on Saturday 26 January 1963. Rather unusually the train is headed by a Stanier class 5 4-6-0 No. 45331 of Bletchley shed, instead of the customary 8F. At this time the country was in the grip of one of the hardest winters of the century, and with the then rather new diesel fleet unable to cope with the low temperatures the large number of extra coal trains required tended to be hauled by any steam engine available.
(G.R. Onley)

129. The sun bursts out momentarily to highlight the exhaust from 9F 2-10-0 No. 92070 as the Leicester-based locomotive takes the Market Harborough branch at Kingsthorpe Mill on Saturday 2 November 1963. In the background the signalman at Northampton No. 5 box makes a note of the passing freight train before settling back in his chair. *(Robin Puryer)*

MOVING THE FREIGHT

130. 'Powering through the mists of time', or at least the mist north of Woodford Halse, this dramatic backlit view of Standard 9F No. 92087 provides a powerful image as it thrashes past with a down non-fitted express freight. Just at the right moment the morning sun has broken through the mist on this day late in November 1960.
(L.H. Cummings)

131. A look from Roade Junction signalbox shows Britannia class No. 70015 APOLLO crossing from fast to slow lines with a deafening noise as the safety valves lift during the operation. The 'Brit' is hauling the 5.13 a.m. Carlisle to Willesden freight train on Saturday 13 Ocotber 1962. With signs of electrification being imminent, the footbridge in the background has already been raised. Roade station is hidden in the background.
(Ian Lyman)

MOVING THE FREIGHT

132. The down 'Burton Empties' clatter their way through Kettering station making good speed behind Stanier Jubilee No. 45610 GHANA with the crew anxious to get back to their home shed on Thursday 18 January 1962. *(Ken Fairey)*

133. 8F class No. 48411 leaves a trail of black smoke as it thrashes through Roade station with a freight train heading for Northampton during August 1961. The distinctive smell of smoke will remain for some minutes after the train has passed for enthusiasts to savour, but to be cursed by local inhabitants. *(L.W. Roy)*

134. *(Above)* The last of the day's sunshine glints off the boiler of Stanier Coronation Pacific No. 46256 SIR WILLIAM A. STANIER, F.R.S. as she steams effortlessly through Roade station with a Euston-bound parcels train on a July evening in 1962. Surprisingly, not one observer is present on the deserted platforms, although children play on the recreation ground in the background. Sadly, no trace of the platforms exists today, although the stationmaster's house, now a private residence, stands boldly at the top of the drive opposite 'The George' public house. *(Roy Sullivan)*

135. *(Left)* What's this — an A4 Pacific hauling a short freight train? Yes, the glory days of the A4 Pacifics hauling top line express passenger trains along the East Coast main line were almost at an end. No. 60006 SIR RALPH WEDGWOOD gently eases through Peterborough North station on Tuesday 13 March 1962 heading towards London. Overhead the sun beams through the steel girder structure of the station roof, creating the unusual effect on the boiler of the A4. *(Ian Lyman)*

136. A remarkable scene on the northern approach to Roade Cutting on Tuesday 26 September 1961. The day has dawned cold and clear, and perfect conditions greet the photographer in time for the passage of Black 5 class No. 45379 with the 9.19 a.m. Rugby to Euston parcels train on the up main line. The cold conditions help to retain the locomotive's 'cotton wool' exhaust which runs the whole length of the train and meets the exhaust from another London-bound train working on the up slow line from Northampton. But, what is the engine working on this train? This is left to the reader's imagination! *(Northampton Chronicle and Echo)*

MOVING THE FREIGHT

137. A deserted Byfield station on the S.M.J. is the setting for a stirring view of Grange class No. 6800 ARLINGTON GRANGE as it shatters the serenity of this little countryside station with a Woodford Halse to Cardiff freight train on Friday 10 January 1964. The locomotive was both internally and externally in poor condition with its front number-plate already missing, and the Cardiff-based locomotive was finally withdrawn a few months later. *(Ian Lyman)*

MOVING THE FREIGHT

138. Hall class No. 7905 FOWEY HALL makes an impressive sight as it bustles through King's Sutton station with a southbound freight on Saturday 8 February 1964. The adjacent fields are white with frost on this beautiful clear sunny winter's morning, but with all the steam leaking out of the locomotive no doubt the driver isn't too happy. Having been based at Banbury shed for the previous four years this regular locomotive was finally withdrawn during the summer of 1964. *(Robin Puryer)*

139. An Annesley 9F No. 92093 heads south from Rugby Central station heading for the Northamptonshire county boundary some two miles away at teatime on Saturday 24 August 1963 on a superb summer's day. This classic view of a 9F on the Great Central with a freight train is so typical of the line in many places. *(J.N. Simms)*

MOVING THE FREIGHT

140. *(Right)* The classic picture of a 9F on a 'windcutter' or Annesley 'runner' almost at journey's end with No. 92095 heading for Woodford Halse with a coal train from Nottingham

The 1 3/4 mile long Catesby tunnel had cabins recessed into the wall near some of its ventilation shafts. These cabins were similar to platelayers' huts containing facilities for the workmen to eat their meals.

The tunnel itself could be a hostile place to work in, for trains working southwards on the rising gradient left the tunnel smokelogged between the ventilation shafts as can be seen in the photograph. Very few trains ran on Sundays when maintenance work was carried out, and without the aid of a northbound train creating the draught to clear the smoke, it could take some time before the bore was clear enough to allow work to continue. *(J. Harrison)*

141. *(Left)* At Rugby Central on a cold crisp sunny morning in February 1955 an Annesley 'runner', made up of returning empty wagons, romps through the station behind class 01 No. 63711 obviously impatient to get back to its home shed.

The 01s were Robinson 2-8-0s that had been rebuilt by Thompson with B1 boilers, and most of them were shedded at Annesley.

In the background an L1 2-6-4 tank shunts an ordinary local passenger train, known to the railwaymen as an 'Ord'. *(J. Harrison)*

142. On a grim wet overcast day 'Dub-dee' No. 90190 from Barrow Hill makes a spectacular attempt to lift its train up the steep gradient in Harbury cutting as it heads towards Banbury on Sunday 5 September 1965. With the engine almost down to crawling pace smoke pours out of the chimney, while steam leaks out of every joint as the driver struggles to keep his engine on the move on the wet rails. *(Derek Smith)*

MOVING THE FREIGHT

143. In the confines of the cutting at the south end of the 1,920 yard long Corby tunnel, Stanier Jubilee No. 45667 JELLICOE moves at walking pace with its train of ballast. Dust and smoke drift out from the entrance as gangs of workmen reballast the tracks within, during September 1962. Like Catesby, this tunnel was on a rising gradient, making southbound trains work hard through the bore, which made working conditions unbearable. On this occasion, however, both lines were closed to rail traffic until the work was completed. *(P.I. Rawlinson)*

144. The footplatemen of Ivatt tank No. 41218 exchange greetings with their colleagues on the footplate of 'Jinty' No. 47273 as the passenger train eases its way towards Wellingborough Midland Road station. The Wellingborough-based 'Jinty' is in the process of shunting the station yard sidings on this April day in 1964. The sidings are now part of the station car park. *(L.H. Cummings)*

MOVING THE FREIGHT

145. On a lovely summer's evening in 1963 a 'Humpy' works the 'Trip' round the curve by Bridge Street Junction signalbox. Both the names were local to Northampton. A 'Humpy' was a Fowler 3F tank, in this case Northampton's No. 47286, and the 'Trip' was the daily freight that transferred wagons between 'Cotton Yards' and 'Down Sidings' ('Down Sidings' being located north of Spencer bridge). In this view from the footbridge that gave access to the shed, 47286 makes steady progress working the last 'Trip' of the day, watched by the footplatemen on Stanier Jubilee No. 45655 KEITH. On returning from 'Down Sidings', 47286 would go to 'Castle Yards' and work the night 'Coal Yard Shunt'. The Jubilee will pull forward over the points and then reverse back on to the shed, with the crew booking on at the signalbox in the process. *(Roy Sullivan)*

146. *(Above)* A 1964 view across 'Cotton Yards' from the C.M.D. (Central Materials Depot) finds a Fowler tank busily performing shunting duties, while in the shed entrance stands a Plasser and Theurer 04 diesel track tamping machine. The C.M.D. is still very much in use today. *(Brian Bibb)*

147. *(Below)* A rarely photographed railway area of Northampton was that between Bridge Street level crossing, in the background, and Hardingstone Junction signalbox. Cotton yard sidings connected with the Central Materials Depot and much shunting work would be carried out in the area. On Sunday 28 April 1963 'Jinty' No. 47653, another Northampton engine, rests in between duties with the houses in Claughton Road in close proximity. Of note is the L.N.W.R. signal post on the right hand side, still in existence at this time. *(Keith Adams)*

MOVING THE FREIGHT

148. Northampton Bridge Street level crossing on Sunday 6 October 1963. The well-known Fowler 'Jinty' class 3F 0-6-0T No. 47499 performs shunting duties in the days when traditional crossing gates and footbridge were to be seen at the location. Hardingstone Junction signalbox can be seen in the distance, while the Northampton Co-operative buildings are in the background. Today the crossing is still very much in use as is the signalbox which is the only working example remaining in Northampton. *(Robin Puryer)*

149. Northampton regular 8F class No. 48658 scurries northwards to Rugby with a breakdown crane from Bletchley on Saturday 19 October 1963 and leaves a smoke trail all the way back to Mill Road bridge near Northampton No. 5 signalbox. The backlighting from the morning sun highlights the steam and smoke to create a very dramatic picture. *(Robin Puryer)*

150. *(Above)* Northampton 4F class 0-6-0 No. 44353 performs shunting duties in the 'Down shunt' at King's Heath on Wednesday morning 21 December 1960, the shortest day. A little winter sunshine reflects off the boiler of the engine as it brings its three oil tanks to the summit of the climb from Northampton No. 4 signalbox. *(Robin Puryer)*

151. *(Right)* After a signal check near Northampton No. 4 signalbox, 8F class No. 48493 struggles to get its mineral train on the move on the evening of Friday 22 May 1964. A permanent way worker strides up the track, and the buildings in the background form part of Pollard Bearings company. On the side of the track, concrete trunking suggests that modernization is just around the corner. *(Keith Adams)*

MOVING THE FREIGHT

152. It is late March 1964 at Kingsthorpe, and the usual long queue of traffic has built up at the closed gates of Boughton level crossing. After a short wait, the driver of the Ford Zodiac witnesses the passage of Standard 9F No. 92126 working hard in moving a heavily loaded ore train in the direction of Market Harborough. Shortly the traffic would be on its way, travelling through the blanket of smoke haze left by the locomotive. *(Roy Sullivan)*

MOVING THE FREIGHT

153. Shrouded in steam from leaking cylinders, and smoking heavily as the fireman spreads a few shovels of coal around the firebox, 'Super D' No. 49342 from Nuneaton shed makes a spectacular sight at Kingsthorpe with a long through freight bound for Rugby. The incredible way the sunshine has lit the exhaust has made the picture particularly dramatic in this 1960 view. The shroud of steam combined with the wheezing noise that the 'Ds' made was known to railwaymen as 'Nor West Asthma'. (L.H. Cummings)

WORKERS AND OBSERVERS

154. A driver and fireman from Peterborough are photographed in the spartan cab of Midland 2-4-0 No. 219 at platform 5 at Northampton Castle station on Saturday 8 December 1934. Life on the footplate conjures up an image of dirt and grime, but for the men who worked there it was often a dedication for life. The cabs frequently gave little or no protection against the elements, but it was pride in their locomotive, and getting the best out of her by using their own skill that was reflected in so many crews. The drivers held an almost enviable position as onlookers crowded around while the locomotive stood at a station. Hopeful children, and even some adults, were always keen to get an invitation onto the footplate. (L. Hanson)

155. *(Left)* A railwayman's job was to serve the community, and this meant working all hours of the day even on public holidays. It is New Year's Eve 1954 and Northampton driver George Quartermain (left) and fireman Colin Lewis, having booked on at Northampton shed at 8.36 p.m., are seen in jovial mood at Castle station ready to take the 9.04 p.m. train to Euston. For George and Colin there will be no New Year celebrations with the family, and after a short break in London they will return with the first newspaper train of 1955 to Northampton, the 2.15 a.m. from Euston. It is all part of a day's work, and for George it would have been one of the hundreds of trips he did in the 35 years of driving he achieved in 45 years of railway service. Colin Lewis later became a driver, and to this day still works on the railway at Northampton, with retirement not far away. *(Northampton Chronicle and Echo)*

156. *(Right)* A happy group of Northampton railwaymen gather round 0-6-0 diesel shunter No. 12089 at Northampton shed in 1966 just before the shed finally closed. Alan Julien and Tom Smith are in the cab of the diesel. From left to right the other men are Ken Beasley, Don Foster, Ken Watts, Stan Braybrook, Bob Kiloh, Walter 'Boggie' Wootton, Barry Ringrose, Ted Baldwin, Ernie Reynolds and Bert Lucas. At the time, Walter Wootton was the local N.U.R. Branch Secretary. *(picture supplied by R.K. Coleman)*

157. *(Right)* At Rugby Midland towards the end of 1951 rebuilt 'Royal Scot' No. 46132 THE KING'S REGIMENT LIVERPOOL stands at the head of an up Holyhead to Euston express. On the platform the driver and footplate inspector stand in discussion, probably about the excessive amount of steam emanating from the locomotive. Only one footplate inspector was employed in each railway district with this particular one being based at Rugby, and easily recognizable by his official uniform of black bowler hat and navy blue overcoat. Many duties were carried out by the inspectors, including travelling with the firemen to test them as 'passed firemen', endeavouring to ride with each driver in his district once every 12 months, investigating persistent late timekeeping and checking on persistent problems with locomotives. *(John G. Click/National Railway Museum)*

158. *(Below)* The footplate inspector watches out for signals at the south end of Rugby station as he takes a trip with the driver and fireman on one of William Stanier's streamlined masterpieces. Painted in crimson lake with gold stripes, No. 6225 DUCHESS OF GLOUCESTER is hauling the up 'Royal Scot' on 4 June 1938. *(L. Hanson)*

159. *(Right)* Walter 'Wally' Blake hard at work in his Bridge Street Junction signalbox during the late 1950s. The signalbox was situated close to Northampton shed, and footplate crew had to book on at the signalbox before their engine was allowed to enter the shed road. Wally was consequently well known by many of the enginemen who worked at Northampton. *(Picture supplied by Mrs J. Surridge)*

160. *(Below)* A single line staff is passed to fireman Leonard Ling as driver Arthur 'Roche' Cherry looks on in their class 8F No. 48445 in 1962 while working a train between Weedon and Southam. Leonard Ling's railway career is typical of so many Northampton-based railwaymen. Born in Far Cotton, he followed the tradition of some of his previous family by working on the railway. He started as a call-up boy, then became a locomotive cleaner, and progressed to a fireman. Finally he became a driver and retired in September 1992 after almost 50 years in the job. The 'Staff' or 'Token' was an essential piece of equipment for single line working, ensuring that only one train could be in the section at a time. *(Picture supplied by Mrs June Ling)*

WORKERS AND OBSERVERS

161. A happy looking Bill Murvin poses for the camera at Brackley station in between his duties as a station porter on a glorious summer's day in June 1962. The three porters who worked at the Great Central station were particularly keen to give a good impression to the travelling public, and took great pride in their work. The station was kept in immaculate condition through their efforts, and was a 'Best Kept Station' competition winner. *(Delmi Battersby)*

162. Amongst the many railway porters who worked in the county there were some who made a name for themselves out of the line of their normal duty. Alonza Weekes, known as 'Lloyd' to his working colleagues, worked at Kettering station in the steam days of the 1960s. In 1962 his observations on the suspicious movements of three dubious characters led to their conviction for stealing property from Kettering station. As a reward he was presented with a cheque for five guineas from the British Transport Commission, and the illustration shows him on the day of the award at Kettering station. His talents also spread to the cricket pitch where he was an excellent player. Later he left the railway to become a postman, and today is well known around the streets of Kettering delivering the mail. *(Evening Telegraph — N.B. Scott collection)*

WORKERS AND OBSERVERS

163.One of the never-ending jobs for footplatemen was filling the water tanks of their locomotives from one of the great variety of water columns to be seen around the different regions.

Here at Brackley on 3 March 1962 Fairburn tank No. 42251 has arrived bunker first with a 'Turnback' from Marylebone. The fireman has 'put the bag in' and the driver makes a final adjustment with the chain before turning on the flow. One assumes the fireman has removed the lamp from the rear of the bunker, and proposes to place it on the top lamp bracket in front of the chimney, a rather precarious operation from on top of the locomotive.

42251 will then run round the coaches to form the 4.55 p.m. train back to Marylebone. *(Delmi Battersby)*

164. and 165. Night shift at Northampton Castle station on 4 April 1962. Much of the town settles down to a peaceful night but, with trains coming and going, parcels arrive in their hundreds and have to be unloaded and sorted to either send off on other trains or be made ready to despatch to areas of the town the next day.

Basil Canham, who appears in both these illustrations, is the platform foreman and supervises the work as parcel trains arrive. Porters George Ratcliffe and Arthur 'Archie' Barker unload one of the vans, while Jan Harte and Walter 'Nobby' Clarke fill their trolley with a similar assortment of parcels from another train. *(Both pictures: Northampton Chronicle and Echo)*

166. Jack Howard, a familiar figure at Northampton Castle in the steam days, stands cheerfully sharing a conversation with the fireman of Neasden-based Standard class No. 76040 which has arrived with a parcels train from Cambridge. Jack, dressed in his usual outfit and carrying his lamp, was one of the train shunters at the station. A dangerous job involving disconnecting pipes between coaches and vans as trains were split, especially at night. Even the rain coming down and making working conditions difficult doesn't seem to bother him during his work on this particular nightshift. *(Northampton Chronicle and Echo)*

167. Scooters were all the rage during the days of the 'Mods and Rockers', with the 'Mods' favouring the scooters. Here at Northampton Castle yards, on Monday 8 April 1957, station staff have loaded a consignment of Lambrettas on to one of the once familier 'Mechanical Horses' for delivery to Norman Stokes' garage. With the Italian Railways having the same standard gauge track as Britain, the railway van carrying the scooters would have travelled across Europe and over the Channel via the train ferry before arriving at Northampton. *(Northampton Chronicle and Echo)*

168. *(Left)* Robert Jones, the parcels office foreman at Northampton Castle station, sets about sorting the piles of parcels in readiness for delivery rounds. A large transfer of goods took place at the station, and in those days anything could be sent by train, from exotic animals to television sets.

On one memorable occasion, a tropical bird arrived for collection by one of the keepers at Wellingborough Zoo. One of the porters decided the bird was hungry and went over to the adjacent warehouse and returned with sprats from a fish train that had arrived earlier from Grimsby. The bird was duly fed and enjoyed the meal. When the keeper arrived and discovered what had happened he was none too pleased and stated that the bird was a vegetarian and had a strict *fruit* diet! *(Northampton Chronicle and Echo)*

169. *(Right)* Arthur 'Archie' Barker is seen working in the telegraph office at Northampton Castle station during a night shift in April 1962. He started on the railway straight from school two years earlier, earning a grand sum of £3.12s.6d a week!

He was a 'jack of all trades' and was happy to do a whole variety of jobs even though his official title was a junior porter. He enjoyed his work so much that even after a 12-hour shift he still wanted to continue instead of going home. Amongst his jobs, he delivered traffic notices to signal boxes, unloaded parcels, helped in the signalbox, and even acted as stationmaster on one occasion.

Once he was sent off to put a fresh oil lamp into one of the semaphore signals at Spencer Bridge, and while at the top of the ladder by the semaphore arm an engine came and stood under the gantry with black smoke belching out of the chimney covering the poor chap. He returned to the station covered in soot from top to toe, much to the amusement of other station staff. He still works at the station in 1992! *(Northampton Chronicle and Echo)*

The Stratford-upon-Avon and Midland Junction Railway employed many well-known characters even in BR times, and one of these was Evan Dines who was based at Towcester station, and towards the end ran it more or less single handed! He was another 'jack of all trades', and these three illustrations show him busy at three different jobs.

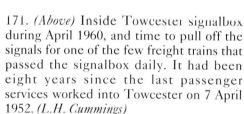

171. *(Above)* Inside Towcester signalbox during April 1960, and time to pull off the signals for one of the few freight trains that passed the signalbox daily. It had been eight years since the last passenger services worked into Towcester on 7 April 1952. *(L.H. Cummings)*

170. *(Left)* On 10 June 1963 he's working in the station office surrounded by the usual amounts of paperwork, files, notices and peeling wall covering! Notice also the incredible design of the telephone, even during this era. *(Northampton Chronicle and Echo)*

172. Next, on to the platform with the rain pouring down to help unload parcels from a pick up freight hauled by class 4F locomotive No. 44522 during the last years of the railway. Freight services were withdrawn on 3 February 1964, with the line and station closing on the same day. Evan Dines was transferred to Northampton Castle as a Station Inspector. *(L.H. Cummings)*

WORKERS AND OBSERVERS

173 and 174. All over the railway system through the county there used to be many signalboxes that were isolated along various routes, in some cases some distance from towns or villages. In many instances the men who worked in these locations were always pleased to see a visitor, and a friendly wave or acknowledgement would normally be followed by an invitation to the box. Then, over a cup of tea, tales of the railway would be related, interrupted by the occasional train that might pass.

These two illustrations show Billing signalbox and Bedford Road crossing box on Monday 25 July 1966. Considering that both boxes were due to close on 21 August 1966, both men look cheerful, with Signalman Alf Busby at Billing, and Crossing Keeper George Martin, gripping his ever present pipe, at Bedford Road. *(Both pictures: Ian Lyman)*

175. Management staff from the Wollaston-based chemical manufacturing company of Scott Bader mingle with British Railway officials on the occasion to mark the export of 350 tons of plasticisers for Hong Kong on Friday 7 August 1964. BRCW Type 2 diesel D5395 stands at the head of the train in Neilsons sidings near Finedon Road signalbox in Wellingborough before departure to London Docks. One wonders how many lorries it would need to carry the same load in this day and age! *(Northampton Chronicle and Echo)*

176. The lampman was the unsung hero on the railway scene, scrambling up and down signal ladders replacing the oil lamps every 7-10 days and cleaning spectacle glasses so that drivers could have a clear sighting of signals. In the days when most signalling was controlled by semaphore signals there were many lampmen. By the time this picture was taken on Thursday 20 November 1986 most of the county's railway system had been modernised and the Midland main line through Kettering and Wellingborough had the honour of still retaining some of the last semaphore signals. Lampman William Causer, a Corby man, performs his duties on the gantry of signals at Finedon Road in Wellingborough and was one of the last lampmen still remaining at work in the area. *(Joe Rajczonek)*

WORKERS AND OBSERVERS

177. Finedon Road signalbox on Saturday 20 September 1986. The day had dawned with a superb sunrise and, after a couple of hours, the warmth of the sunshine beats through the windows of the signalbox.

Signalman Ron Griffin takes the opportunity, in between trains, to clean the windows. The sun highlights the wooden nameboard as well as the neglected paintwork on the wooden panels. Modernisation was just around the corner, and within 15 months the box was to be made redundant, therefore the run-down had already started.

However, Ron Griffin, a railwayman all his working life, kept up the traditions of a professional signalman right up to the time the box finally closed on 5 December 1987 when he retired. Always a gentleman, he welcomed many railway folk into the box with a smile, a cup of tea and a chat. Like many of the thousands of signalmen who used to work on the railway, he is part of a lost era. *(Joe Rajczonek)*

178. With the level crossing gates at Bridge Street station having been damaged the previous evening in a car accident, a flagman armed with his red flag controls the traffic. In the pouring rain a work-stained class 8F locomotive approaches heading towards Wellingborough on Saturday 23 January 1960. A flagman at such a busy crossing as this was an extremely rare occurence. Passengers in the Yorks Bros coach look with interest at the scene through the misted-up coach windows. Incredibly, some 32 years later the buildings in the background still exist, as does the 'Cotton End' street nameplate, and the Old White Hart Inn in the background will be remembered by railwaymen as the place where the local NUR meetings were held. *(Northampton Chronicle and Echo)*

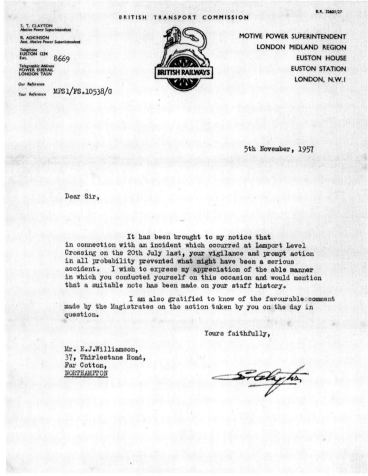

BRITISH TRANSPORT COMMISSION

B.R. 32601/27

S. T. CLAYTON
Motive Power Superintendent

B. ADKINSON
Asst. Motive Power Superintendent

Telephone
EUSTON 1234
Ext. 8669

Telegraphic Address
POWER EUSRAIL
LONDON TASN

Our Reference

Your Reference MPS1/FS.10538/G

MOTIVE POWER SUPERINTENDENT
LONDON MIDLAND REGION
EUSTON HOUSE
EUSTON STATION
LONDON, N.W.1

5th November, 1957

Dear Sir,

      It has been brought to my notice that in connection with an incident which occurred at Lamport Level Crossing on the 20th July last, your vigilance and prompt action in all probability prevented what might have been a serious accident. I wish to express my appreciation of the able manner in which you conducted yourself on this occasion and would mention that a suitable note has been made on your staff history.

      I am also gratified to know of the favourable comment made by the Magistrates on the action taken by you on the day in question.

      Yours faithfully,

Mr. E.J.Williamson,
37, Thirlestane Road,
Far Cotton,
NORTHAMPTON

179, 180 and 181. This remarkable scene at the level crossing at Lamport station resulted from a confrontation between ex W.D. class No. 90103 and a coach about 4.30 a.m. on the foggy morning of 20 July 1957. Driver Edgar Williamson and his fireman Teddy Tinker were on the light engine proceeding towards Market Harborough when, as they approached the level crossing, driver Williamson noticed that a bus had crashed through the crossing gates. In the seconds available he applied the brakes and slowed the locomotive down to a walking pace before it hit the coach, turning it on to the opposite track. Driver Williamson alerted signalboxes in both directions, and fortunately no one was hurt. Although no one could be certain, it was widely believed that the coach driver had fallen asleep at the wheel seconds before the accident occurred. A letter of commendation was later sent to Edgar Williamson by the Superintendent of British Railways.

182. Permanent way work of a complex nature was carried out by the 'Relaying Gangs', each gang consisting of around 24 men including at least one 'Lookout Man'. At Northampton Castle on Sunday 1 October 1961 the two large steam cranes from Willesden assist the 'Relaying Gang' in replacing the huge 16" wide by 14" deep longitudinal timbers to the bridge on the up line to Roade. The 'workers' watch intently during a vital stage in the proceedings, while the 'observers' seem to have lost interest altogether. *(W.J.S. Meredith)*

183. *(Left)* Here we see a 'Lookout Man' on duty at Northampton, just south of West Bridge during May 1964. He will already have warned the 'Relaying Gang' of the imminent arrival of the train by blowing the horn. His red, green and yellow flags are rolled up on the adjacent box ready for use in case of emergency, and he must have at least six warning detonators in his possession ready to place on the line. Stanier 8F No. 48334 from Kirkby-in-Ashfield leaks steam profusely while easing past with an up freight. *(Tony Foster)*

184. *(Below)* General permanent way work was performed by 'Platelayers' or 'Slip and Drainage' gangs. In this fine study a gang takes a break for lunch while performing maintenance work at an unknown location in the county during the 1930s. These gangs would consist of a Ganger, Sub Ganger and three or four platelayers who would be men local to the area. One of the first jobs when reaching the site was to light the all-important fire, fuel for which had to be obtained from the immediate surroundings. Then coal thrown down by locomen from passing trains helped keep the fire going. The men are using salt-glazed drainage pipes as seats, and it is interesting to see that all of them have wicker food baskets. During the 1950s Rugby District had an entire gang of women platelayers whose jobs included weeding and other less physical duties. *(W.J.S. Meredith)*

185 and 186. A large group of permanent way and other railwaymen gather as the lifting of 'Mogul' class No. 43048 takes place. Surprisingly, normal trains are still being allowed to pass, and rebuilt Royal Scot class No. 46162 QUEEN'S WESTMINSTER RIFLEMAN crawls by with a Manchester-bound express.

The accident occurred some 500 yards north of Kettering station on Monday 18 January 1960. Eight wagons from a Clay Cross to Wellingborough freight train began to derail about 100 yards before the accident site. No. 43048 was working the 6.33 a.m. local train from Kettering to Leicester and collided with the wagons, causing the locomotive to fall on to its side.

Fireman Harry Ford had to run down the track at the time to stop an on-coming freight train. Driver Herbert Jackson, also escaped but suffered facial injuries. Fortunately, apart from this, no one else was injured. *(Both pictures: Tony Heighton)*

WORKERS AND OBSERVERS

187. Workers and observers look on as 8F class No. 48616 is lifted in the process of being rerailed on Sunday 31 July 1960 while Geoff Dentith, the Assistant Motive Power Superintendant at the time, photographs the scene. The accident occurred on 17 June 1960 at a remote location about half a mile from Turvey on the Northampton to Bedford branch line. Although double track, the line between Olney and Turvey was operated as a single line for some years, with the other line being used to store coaches. On the day of the accident No. 48616, hauling a train of pre-fab track towards Northampton, was allowed to enter this section of line to permit the passage of a troop train in the opposite direction. Unfortunately, because of a misunderstanding, instead of stopping the driver continued for about a mile before colliding with the stationary coaches. Luckily both driver Dick Wooding and fireman Bill Watkins jumped clear before impact, and survived. The locomotive, which had careered down the embankment, did not and became the first of its class to be withdrawn. *(Ken Fairey)*

WORKERS AND OBSERVERS

188 and 189. At about 4 a.m. on the morning of Wednesday 3 July 1963 another railway accident occurred on the Midland main line about one mile north of Glendon and Rushton station.

'Peak' class diesel D49 was travelling down the steep gradient towards Kettering with the 12.05 a.m. night express from Manchester Central to St Pancras when it ran into the stationary 1.00 a.m. Birmingham to Brent freight train.

The train was hit with such force that D49 and the first two coaches were derailed. Only two people were injured, one of those being the secondman on D49. The wooden bodied vans in the photograph were severely damaged, and the railway workers faced with the awesome task of clearing up survey the wreckage.

D49 survived the accident and two years later was named THE MANCHESTER REGT before being finally withdrawn in December 1980. *(Northampton Chronicle and Echo)*

190. Another serious railway accident took place on the Northampton to Bedford branch just after Oakley Junction about two miles north of Bedford station on Friday afternoon 21 January 1938. The 2.10 p.m. St Pancras to Bradford express, hauled by Jubilee class No. 5568 WESTERN AUSTRALIA, was travelling at about 60 mph hauling its seven coaches with some 150 people on board when it took the Northampton branch instead of continuing along the main line. Hughes/Fowler 'Crab' class No. 2893 had been shunting coaching stock and was standing on the branch at the front of 20 coaches. 5568 then collided with 2893 head on, and the horrifying crash could be heard for some distance. Miraculously only one person was killed, although several were injured. 24 hours later, on the Saturday afternoon, schoolboys sift through the wreckage, while other observers look at the damaged Jubilee as an eerie atmosphere is created by the smouldering remains of the wreckage. *(L. Hanson)*

191. A typical scene at the south end of Rugby Midland station on Saturday 5 May 1962. The station was a mecca for trainspotters of all ages, especially at weekends and after school on schooldays. For a Saturday it's remarkable how many of the spotters in this picture are in school uniform! With many named locomotives, as well as numerous other types that passed through the station, there was never a dull moment. On this occasion it is Cup Final day, although the Princess Royal No. 46208

PRINCESS HELENA VICTORIA is hauling a Llandudno to Euston train departing at 1.28 p.m. with Northampton the next stop. Water is being added to 46208's tender, while the spotters compare notes and generally wait in anticipation for the next arrival. The small hut in the background was built to provide shelter for footplate crews waiting to take over for southbound trains. On many occasions trainspotters would shelter in the hut and share tales with the enginemen. *(J.N. Simms)*

WORKERS AND OBSERVERS

The stretch of line from Gayton signalbox to the road bridge just north of Blisworth station was a favourite for many trainspotters in the Northampton area. Armed with duffle bags full of 'goodies' many would cycle from the surrounding area, including Northampton, to sit by the lineside and watch the never-ending stream of trains pass through. The expresses would really thrash past, and the excitement created as one of these could be heard approaching was something that will always be remembered. Whether it was a 'Jubilee' or a 'Duchess', someone would shout out and then, after the spectacle of the passing train, much celebration would follow if in fact the locomotive was a 'cop', or conversely cries of 'not that old crate again' for an engine that was a common visitor.

192. *(Above)* A summer Saturday brings out the spotters on 30 August 1958 with Jubilee class No. 45738 SAMSON hurtling past with a Euston to Wolverhampton express on a superb summer's day. *(L. Hanson)*

193. *(Right)* On another occasion in 1949 the tremendous speed of rebuilt Patriot No. 45531 SIR FREDERICK HARRISON is too much for the camera as it heads south with an express watched by another group of spotters, including the cycling brigade. *(Robin Freeston)*

The classic trainspotter in the steam days was a common sight either on station platforms or out in the countryside. On school days it was almost a ritual to go off to the lineside after school, still dressed in full school uniform, including school cap, blazer and satchel! During other times the old duffle bag would appear, filled with sandwiches, a bottle of Tizer, notebook, pens and, of course, a copy of the Ian Allan 'abc'.

194 and 195. These two scenes at Peterborough North station on Saturday 25 August 1962 show that the spotters are out in force. The famous A3 class Pacific No. 60103 FLYING SCOTSMAN waits with a down train in mid-afternoon with spotters littering the platform. A group of them take interest in what seems to be a problem with the locomotive, whilst others relax and write another number into their notebooks. Station pilot N2 class No. 69583 from the local New England shed shunts wagons under the watchful eye of three young admirers. Shorts and sandals were obviously the style at the time, being far more suitable than the tracksuits and trainers of today! *(Both pictures: J.N. Simms)*

196. *(Top)* Standard class 5 No. 75056 runs past Wellingborough locoshed and prepares to stop at Wellingborough Midland Road station with a local train from Leicester on Saturday 18 July 1959. Some of the youngsters in the foreground stop their games and gaze over to the train, whilst others continue as if the train doesn't exist. Well, it is only a local train, the engine of which they have probably seen many times. *(Robin Puryer)*

197. *(Bottom)* The draw of Rugby is once again evident as no fewer than 28 trainspotters are gathered on a summer Saturday to watch the numerous passing trains. This particular location was especially popular because two main lines could be viewed — the West Coast and the Great Central. In between the predominantly steam-hauled trains, diesels 10000/10001 growl past with the up 'Royal Scot' on a sunny hot 20 June 1959. Surprisingly to some, 10000/10001 made their debut together on the West Coast main line some 11 years earlier in October 1948 and hauled the 'Royal Scot' for a demonstration run in June 1949! *(Robin Puryer)*

WORKERS AND OBSERVERS

199. Two young trainspotters stand on West Bridge overlooking a deserted Northampton Castle station waiting for the next train to arrive. Even on this cold winter's day nothing would keep them away from their obsession with engine numbers. *(Northampton Chronicle and Echo)*

198. At last the long summer holidays have arrived, and the local trainspotters at Northampton head for Victoria Park and to the railway line. The regular spot, the raised seat by the fence, is already well occupied, but with work being carried out by the side of the railway there is a rare opportunity to clamber on to building materials to view the trains. Sulzer Type 2 D5025 brings a local train out of Castle station and heads for Rugby, while 'Sputnik' D2903 performs shunting duties on the left. Steam, however, is still very much in evidence, with at least four locomotives in the background in this scene on Monday 23 July 1962. *(Robin Puryer)*

200. *(Left)* Platform No. 1 at Castle station, and a group of young trainspotters waiting for their London-bound train have the opportunity to begin their quota of engine numbers for the day in the shape of class 5 4-6-0 No. 45448 which accelerates past with a short freight train on Saturday 31 August 1963. No doubt the trip to London would have been talked about all week, and the chance to fill page after page with many new steam locomotive numbers was a great incentive to save up that pocket money for the trip south! *(Robin Puryer)*

201. *(Below)* Sadly it is the last day of passenger services to Bedford on a cold and damp Saturday 3 March 1962. Nevertheless, a busy scene on platform 5 at Northampton Castle station, with the bustle of passengers and footplate crew before departure. Steam leaks freely out of the front end of Ivatt 2-6-2 tank No. 41225 as a young trainspotter in full school uniform waits expectantly for the next arrival, and hopefully a new number to put into his huge notebook. *(L. Hanson)*

202. The absence of wooden panels out of the fence adjacent to Northampton locomotive shed allows the photographer's daughters, Diane and Jeanette, to stand precariously and watch the movement of class 8F 2-8-0 No. 48020 on the Blisworth line. The photographer, a railwayman at the time, would take his daughters to the shed many times to see the locomotives, and it shows that not only little boys were interested in steam locomotives. Unfortunately, the steam era in Northampton had only a few more months remaining when this picture was taken on Saturday 27 March 1965. Perhaps in years to come they may just have remembered the old steam engines. *(George Smith)*

WORKERS AND OBSERVERS

203. A poignant reminder of wartime Britain, with evacuees arriving at Northampton Castle station from London during August 1941. Most of the children appear to be remarkably cheerful considering the fact that they have left their families. No doubt the appearance of a photographer has intrigued them as they file down the station platform wondering what to expect in their temporary new homes in the town. *(Northampton Record Office)*

204. Robert Brothers circus arrives at Kettering station on Sunday 24 April 1955 for its annual visit, and the station staff join in the spirit of the occasion before the procession of animals through the town. Station foreman Norman Scott (left) and head passenger shunter Ray Roworth (middle) sit on top of the elephant with porter Joe Orth, while goods yard inspector H. Lindsay stands in front of them. The arrival of the elephants at the station was always met with amusement. Whenever they were upset they used to violently shake the railway van they travelled in, and on being led out of the van down the platform they would try to get hold of anything in their path. At one time a porter's bicycle, inadvertently left on the platform, was thrown to one side by one of the elephants! Robert Brothers representatives in the photograph are Jock Holmes (right) and a young Bobby Robert, relative of the proprietor. (*Northamptonshire Advertiser — N.B. Scott collection*)

WORKERS AND OBSERVERS

205. Chipperfield's Circus comes to town! Crowds of people of all ages surround the concourse at Castle station as the circus departs on its procession through the streets of the town to the show site on Sunday 7 October 1962. The sight of the 'high wire' star perched on her swing has some of the children in the crowd stunned in amazement. Always a popular occasion with Northampton folk, and a chance to see all the animals and performers before going to the actual show in the coming week. *(Northampton Chronicle and Echo)*

DOWN BY THE LOCO SHED

Arguably the most evocative sight for all steam enthusiasts had to be a shed full of steam engines. The sight and sound of the engines surrounded by the swirling smoke and steam created a marvellous atmosphere which is remembered nostalgically by trainspotters and also by many of the men who worked in them. Dirty, dark and smoky places they were, but the sheds were filled with the true spirit and adventure of the railway. The illustrations in this spread show some of that magic atmosphere.

206. Banbury shed on a very cold January day in 1965, with columns of steam and smoke hanging in the cold still air, darkening the sky above. The ever present cloud of smoke risng around any shed site conveyed the steam age atmosphere very strongly. *(Ian Krause)*

207. A remarkable view from the coaling stage at Woodford Halse with a wonderful variety of locomotives, all simmering ready for their next turn of duty. W.D. class No. 90474, V2 class No. 60961 and 60963, Stanier 'Mogul' class No. 42961 and Standard class 4 No. 76052 are just some of the locomotives present. Sunday 3 March 1963 is the date of the occasion, with things gradually getting back to normal after the severe winter. *(Delmi Battersby)*

To wander around a locomotive shed, whether officially or unofficially, was a delight. For trainspotters it was a chance to fill a page full of numbers that otherwise may have taken many hours to obtain spotting on the lineside. The anticipation of finding a rare engine on the shed made one come back time after time, and to walk by the side of these huge steam locomotives was quite an experience. Then, at the end of each visit, to come away with that characteristic unforgettable smell of steam and oil clinging to one's clothes. Those were the days!

208. On the afternoon of Sunday 16 July 1961 Ivatt class 2 2-6-2 No. 41278 and Fowler class 4 2-6-4T No. 42381 bask in the summer sunshine at Northampton shed.

Being parked at the outer end of their road, they were obviously booked for late Sunday evening or early Monday morning duties. No. 41278 had been a recent addition to the Northampton allocation and was a welcome change to the twins 41218 and 41219, which probably still haunt the site of the shed!

Even when 41278 was withdrawn the following year it still carried the 'lion on the bike' emblem. *(G.R. Onley)*

DOWN BY THE LOCO SHED

209. The familiar choking yellow smoke from a freshly lit fire begins to crawl out of the chimney of Jubilee class No. 45643 RODNEY and spreads to other parts of Northampton shed like a creeping fog, creating an atmosphere only to be found at a locoshed. The green liveried Jubilee pokes out of road ten looking quite resplendent amongst the usual freight and shunting locomotives normally resident at the shed. For local enthusiasts the 'namer' from Crewe is a bonus on this Sunday afternoon 11 November 1962. An admirer has written 'clean me please' in chalk on the running plate near the cylinders, even though the locomotive looks reasonably clean. *(George Smith)*

210. On Sunday 14 October 1962 an enthusiast's special returning via Market Harborough, Northampton and Bedford was due to be hauled through to St Pancras by one of the last two surviving unrebuilt Patriot 4-6-0s. On arrival at Northampton Castle station 'authority' decreed that the engine could not be used over the Northampton to Bedford branch. This stroke of luck resulted in No. 45543 HOME GUARD of Carnforth shed being replaced by a Northampton class 5 and going on to the shed for servicing. This gave the opportunity for photographers to rush down to the shed to attempt, without tripods, to photograph the locomotive! One example is shown here, and this was the last time an unrebuilt Patriot visited Northampton, with its final departure on a freight train to Warrington on 16 October 1962. (*Brian Denny*)

DOWN BY THE LOCO SHED

Conditions in most locomotive sheds were normally very dark and cramped, making photography almost impossible. Very little room to use a tripod resulted in hand-held exposures, and nine times out of ten these failed. However, the two views here, inside Northampton shed, not only have worked but are quite unique.

211. *(Above)* A most unusual visitor to the shed on Sunday 11 November 1962 was EE Type 4 diesel No. D334 which had failed the previous day at Blisworth while hauling the up 'Royal Scot', to be replaced by class 5 No. 45302 from Northampton shed. D334 was towed to Northampton with its headboard still mounted on its front! Notice how the photographer has had to clamber on to one of the adjacent locos to be able to have enough room to take this rare photograph. *(George Smith)*

212. *(Right)* News that something unusual was down at the shed spread amongst local enthusiasts on Tuesday 12 June 1962. On this occasion the photographer ventured down, and sure enough a rare intruder from Doncaster shed, Gresley class O2 No. 63981, which apparently had worked to Northampton on a freight train, was very much present on shed. *(Robin Puryer)*

There was always something special about a locomotive that carried a name, and the anticipation of seeing a named locomotive at a locoshed always generated a lot of excitement amongst enthusiasts, especially if the locomotive wasn't expected. Around the county, named locomotives were commonplace at Peterborough (New England), Rugby and Banbury, but less so at Northampton, Wellingborough, Kettering and Woodford Halse. Many enthusiasts would no doubt have admired the nameplates on the locomotives as they visited these sheds, and probably have wondered where the names originated. There was, of course, an immense range of variety in the choice of a name for a locomotive, and a handful of examples are illustrated.

213. *(Left)* Thompson 4-6-2 A2/1 class No. 60508 DUKE OF ROTHESAY makes an imposing sight as it stands at its home shed of New England at Peterborough on Tuesday 19 April 1960. The locomotive was named after David Stewart, son of Robert III of Scotland who was made the Duke of Rothesay in 1399. *(Ken Fairey)*

214. *(Below)* The impressive streamlined shape of Gresley A4 class Pacific No. 60005 SIR CHARLES NEWTON is very prominent as the engine is prepared for its next duty at Peterborough (New England) shed on Saturday 24 August 1963. The locomotive's first name was CAPERCAILLE after a Scottish game bird, and this was superseded by CHARLES H. NEWTON one of the Directors of the L.N.E.R. in the 1940s who later became SIR CHARLES NEWTON. *(Robin Puryer)*

215. A Sunday afternoon visit to Northampton shed in September 1962 offers the superb sight of Aston-based Britannia Pacific No. 70043 LORD KITCHENER standing out amongst the mundane freight locomotives. Horatio Herbert Kitchener, 1st Earl Kitchener of Khartoum, was an English soldier and statesman who was made Secretary of War in 1914. *(George Smith)*

DOWN BY THE LOCO SHED

216. Wellingborough shed was renowned for the many Standard class 9Fs that were allocated to it to work the many freight trains in the area. This view, photographed unusually from inside a wagon, on Sunday 29 April 1962 shows six examples in various positions in the yard by Wellingborough North signalbox. In the foreground locomotive 92132, 92025 and 92159, all looking somewhat work stained, stand at rest. *(Ken Fairey)*

Unless a locomotive shed was situated in a convenient triangle of lines which enabled locomotives to be turned, then an essential piece of equipment was the turntable, whether it be situated outside, as at Blisworth, or in the centre of a roundhouse, as at Wellingborough.

217. *(Right)* The Stratford-upon-Avon and Midland Junction Railway turntable at Blisworth accommodates Johnson Midland 2F No. 3677 which is slowly being swung round by her crew on Wednesday 22 March 1933. In this unique photograph the small S.M.J. single road engine shed still stands between the turntable and signal box, while the locomotive is painted in the 1923 to 1928 black goods livery, with the number on the tender and L.M.S. in a vermilion panel on the cab side. The engine shed was taken down and re-erected at Towcester for use as a store for cattle feed. *(W.J.S. Meredith)*

218. *(Left)* Johnson class 2 0-6-0 No. 58148 stands on the turntable inside Wellingborough No. 2 shed on Tuesday 8 May 1962. At the time this vintage locomotive was one of only three that were still running in normal service, and all were based at Coalville shed. It had come to Wellingborough for front end attention to cylinders and valves prior to working a railtour over the Westbridge branch in Leicester. *(Ken Fairey)*

DOWN BY THE LOCO SHED

219 (Above) A fine side-on study of Churchwood class 8F 2-8-0 No. 2856 catching the last of the winter light as it rests by the front of the four road shed. The locomotive shed at Banbury was literally a stone's throw from the Northamptonshire boundary and was finally closed in October 1966. (J.N. Simms)

220. (Below) The first day of December 1962 and a wander around Banbury shed reveals a typical G.W. array of locomotives. 'Hall' class No. 6904 CHARFIELD HALL and 'Modified Hall' class No. 7905 FOWEY HALL both displaying the Banbury shed code of 84C on their smokeboxes, stand side by side with a glimpse of the main Paddington-Birmingham main line in the background. (J.N. Simms)

221. New England locomotive shed at Peterborough on Thursday 16 May 1963 plays host to two visiting locos, Thompson B1 class 4-6-0 No. 61135 from Doncaster and Gresley O2 class No. 63974 from Grantham. New England-based loco Gresley A3 class Pacific No. 60108 GAY CRUSADER, looking a little worse for wear, hides in the background. No doubt, being a working day, all three are being serviced ready for more action later, while one of the shed staff clears away the endless piles of ash from cleaned out locomotive fireboxes. *(Ken Fairey)*

DOWN BY THE LOCO SHED

Down by the Loco Shed

For the local railwaymen and steam enthusiasts in Northampton the illustrations here will bring the memories flooding back of the good old days at Northampton locomotive shed.

222. *(Above)* April 1963, and the afternoon sunlight picks out the smokeboxes of the line up of locomotives, with Derby-based Jubilee class No. 45610 GHANA being surrounded by the more common Black 5s and 8F. Northampton Black 5 4-6-0 No. 44682 on the left, and 8F class No. 48479 from Willesden, and Black 5 No. 45493 from Rugby to the right. *(Neil Hodson)*

223. *(Left)* What is this, a 'V2' on the shed? The extremely rare intruder from the Eastern Region No. 60871 in poor external condition stands impatiently amongst the more familiar L.M.S. engines on Sunday 14 July 1963. Not to let the occasion go by without celebration, the locomotive was rostered the following morning for the 8.17 a.m. train to London Euston and 12.10 p.m. return. In fact this happened a number of times that week before the locomotive finally returned to its home shed at New England. *(Robin Puryer)*

224. Freight locomotives predominate on the roads at Northampton shed in this panoramic view from the top of the coaling plant one Sunday afternoon in the summer of 1957. On the line adjacent to the shed, a down train diverted via Blisworth comes into view headed by 'Baby Scot' No. 45518 BRADSHAW. *(J. Stewart)*

Down by the Loco Shed

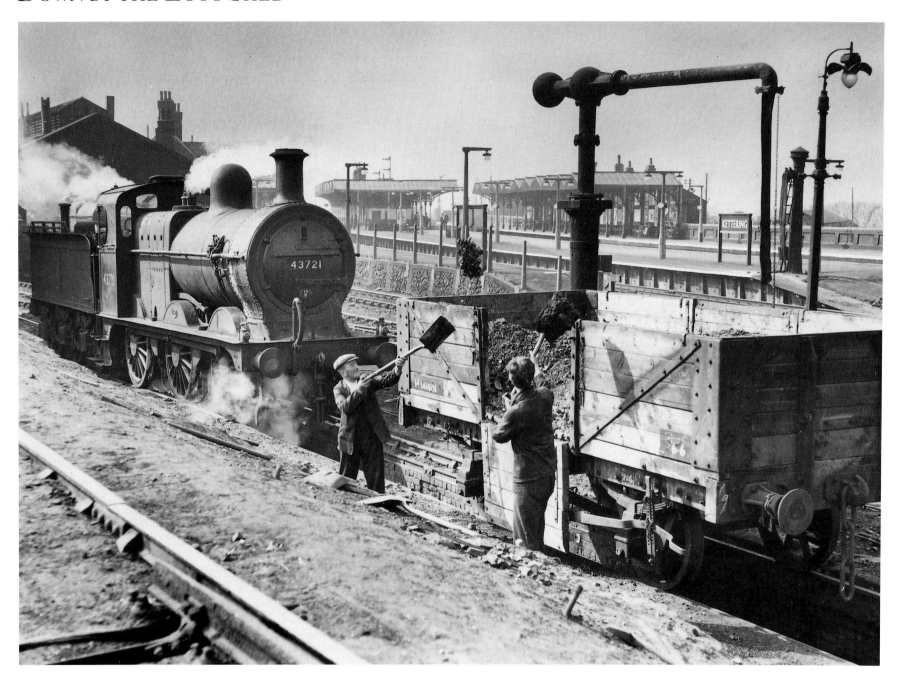

225. Midland 3F 0-6-0 No. 43721 stands in the warm sunshine at its home shed of Kettering watching over two shed staff who are busily disposing of ash. This backbreaking job, although unpopular, was a vital part of shed life. In the background is a superb view of Kettering station showing the close proximity of the shed to the end of platform 2. This of course made it more interersting for the platform observers to watch the various movements in the shed yard. The date is Saturday 30 May 1959. (*R.C. Riley*)

226. Transferring to the end of Platform 2 at Kettering station produced this excellent view of Kettering shed on 7 August 1954, with three different types of locomotives in residence. From left to right: Standard class 2 2-6-0 No. 78028, veteran ex-G.E.R. JI5 class No. 65390 and Fowler 2-6-2T No. 40022. The four road Midland shed built in 1876 had arched openings with very limited clearances, hence the whitewashed areas painted on the shed walls as shown. On the right the station buildings are visible, and even today they are still mostly unchanged, although the shed area has been replaced by a car park. *(R.M. Tomkins)*

227. A rare glimpse inside Rugby Locomotive Repair Works on Sunday 28 October 1934 finds a Fowler 2-6-2 tank No. 18 in company with one of George Whale's 19" 4-6-0 goods, a 'Prince of Wales' 4-6-0 and an 0-6-2 coal tank in different stages of overhaul or repair. The works, situated near the running shed off Mill Road, was an important facility, allowing attention to be given to locomotives arriving from over a wide area, the coal tanks from South Wales being regular visitors. *(W.J.S. Meredith)*

228. A remarkable image of harnessed power inside Rugby Testing Station as the motion of Stanier Coronation Pacific No. 46225 DUCHESS OF GLOUCESTER travels at very high speed during one of the 76 test runs carried out on the locomotive between 31 January and 16 May 1955. The locomotive is running on rollers, and has its drawbar attached to a hydraulic cylinder which was itself held in position by a steel and concrete structure weighing some 3,000 tons. Delayed 10 years by the war, the testing station came into use in 1948 and enabled staff to make scientific analysis of a locomotive's output and efficiency under closely monitored and controlled conditions, thus gaining much information to assist in any future development of the steam locomotive. The footplate crews from the local shed tried to avoid working at the station as they did not like being under such close scrutiny. *(John G. Click/National Railway Museum)*

INDUSTRIAL ACTION

229. An aerial view, in 1935, of the Wellingborough Ironworks complex scoured out of the rural Northamptonshire countryside while the works was in process of being rebuilt. Although the first blast furnace was put into production in 1886 the trade depression in the early 1930s closed the ironworks and tramway in 1932.

After this a working agreement with Stanton and Wellingborough Iron Companies resulted in a complete rebuilding of the ironworks on modern lines and changes to improve the efficiency of the ironstone railway. In the photograph Finedon Road can be seen in the immediate foreground, with a solitary vehicle, while Finedon Road signalbox hides behind a rake of wagons. Opposite to the signalbox the railway entrance from the Midland Railway to the works can be seen, and standing by the weighbridge near this point is one of the standard gauge industrial locomotives that worked within the works.

The narrow gauge line that ran from the works to the quarries can be seen on the right passing via a tunnel underneath the Midland Railway. Wellingborough South Sidings signalbox stands above the tunnel exit on the far right. *(Picture provided by H.E. Storr)*

230. Peckett built 0-6-0ST, later to be numbered No. 87, brings a load of empty wagons from Wellingborough ironworks via the short tunnel in the summer of 1959. A London to Manchester express conveniently passes at the same time. The imposing structure of the ironworks dominates the background. The tunnel under the B.R. main line was built of a narrow bore, and consequently a notice warning employees to wait 'until the smoke has cleared' was displayed. Also provided as extra protection were colour signals which changed from green to red by a track-circuit arrangement on the approach of a locomotive. The ironworks finally closed at the end of October 1962. *(Tony Heighton)*

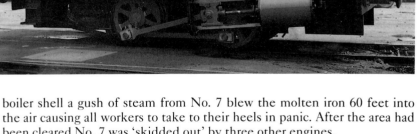

231 and 232. Andrew Barclay built 0-4-0ST No. 7 which arrived new at Wellingborough Ironworks in 1941 was involved in a horrific accident in 1956.

On this unique occasion No. 7 was shunting hot metal ladles under the blast furnace plant when a stream of 100 tons of molten iron and slag broke out at a temperature of 1,200 degrees C and crashed onto the top of the locomotive! As the molten iron burned its way through everything to the boiler shell a gush of steam from No. 7 blew the molten iron 60 feet into the air causing all workers to take to their heels in panic. After the area had been cleared No. 7 was 'skidded out' by three other engines.

Amazingly the locomotive was repaired despite extensive boiler and cylinder damage and the total cost was about half that of a new locomotive. The illustrations show No. 7 before and after the repair. *(Pictures provided by H.E. Storr)*

233. The railway system linking Wellingborough quarries with the ironworks was the last narrow gauge steam worked line in the ironstone industry to close in the autumn of 1966.

Two Peckett 0-6-0 were built new for the line in 1934 and a third added in 1942. All three are visible at the locomotive shed at Wellingborough on Saturday 19 September 1964. No. 85 receives attention from fitters while No. 86 occupies the shed building and No. 87 waits on a train of wagons. Fortunately all three locos were saved from the scrapyard and today can be viewed at the Irchester Narrow Gauge Railway museum in Irchester Country Park. No. 85 has the distinguished honour of being the only steam locomotive in the county at present to be in active use. *(Trevor Riddle)*

One of the most popular industrial railway systems to be visited in the county was the Kettering Furnaces complex situated on the outskirts of Kettering. Narrow gauge Victorian built steam locomotives hauling wooden wagons created a scene of real old-fashioned character in the rural Northamptonshire countryside.

234. *(Above)* Rothwell Lodge Pit, about two miles from the furnaces, was one of the last to be quarried. This picture was taken during the winter of 1959 shows KETTERING FURNACES No. 7 waiting with steam to spare while its train is loaded with ore. The six-coupled Manning Wardle locomotives were introduced to supersede the four-coupled examples to cope with the steep gradients on the line from the quarries to the furnaces. *(Tony Heighton)*

235. *(Right)* KETTERING FURNACES No. 2, built by Black and Hawthorn in 1879, stands simmering during the summer of 1958 while wagons of ore are unloaded. The four-coupled locomotives were confined to marshalling duties at the furnaces where the wooden side-tipping wagons used to be fly-shunted on to the elevated 'dock'. From here the load of ore was discharged into a clamp below for calcining. When burnt, the ore was taken by dumper to a hoist for lifting into the furnace. *(Tony Heighton)*

INDUSTRIAL ACTION

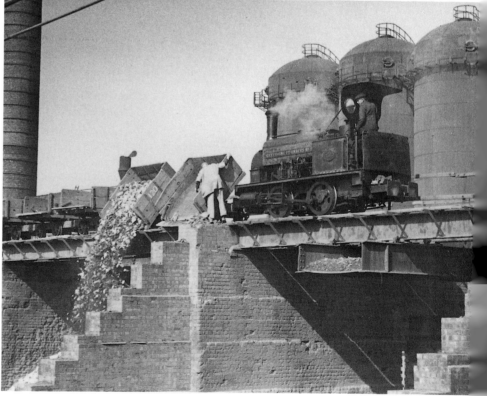

236. A superbly rural view of KETTERING FURNACES No. 7, built by Manning Wardle in 1897, setting off with empty wagons past the weighbridge at the furnaces during a glorious summer's day in 1958. It was settings such as this that made the industrial railways so quaint and charming. *(Tony Heighton)*

238. (Above) Geddington viaduct situated near the old Geddington station on the Kettering to Corby main line forms an interesting background as No. 44 CONWAY heads off to Corby with iron ore from Rothwell West Pit. To reach the point where the iron ore was loaded into wagons the ore was carried via an aerial ropeway system that was almost six miles in length. It was only opened for four years between 1959 and 1963. 'CONWAY' an 0-6-0ST built by Kitson in 1933 in its usual splendid external condition survived the scrapman and is now preserved. *(Tony Heighton)*

237. *(Facing page)* This classic 1958 view of the Kettering Furnaces industrial railway in the rural Northamptonshire landscape is quite delightful. On the 'main line' between the quarries and the furnaces KETTERING FURNACES No. 7 makes a superb sight as it chugs towards Kettering with the train wagons rocking and lurching at all different angles on a clear sunny December day. The main A6 road between Rothwell and Kettering is situated just off the left of the photograph, and the bridge in the background carries a minor road from the A6 to Glendon Hall. *(Tony Heighton)*

INDUSTRIAL ACTION

239. It is just after Christmas on Monday 28 December 1964 with snow very much in evidence as a Hudswell Clarke built 0-6-0ST locomotive of 1895 vintage sweeps round the curve with a train of iron ore from the quarry at Desborough. The view is seen from the minor road that joins Desborough with Pipewell. The quarries and railway were owned by the Sheepbridge Company, and iron ore used to go Sheepbridge works. The locomotive was originally named SHEEPBRIDGE No. 25. *(Trevor Riddle)*

INDUSTRIAL ACTION

240. The same train proceeds across the icy minor road at a deserted unmanned crossing as it continues its way to Desborough sidings. This part of the line was opened as late as 1957, but by December 1966 the whole system had closed. The locomotive continued to the end and was then preserved. *(Trevor Riddle)*

241. No. 32, a shabby looking example of one of the many Hawthorn Leslie locomotives at Corby Steelworks, shunts lime containers outside Lloyds Sidings South signalbox during March 1971. With Corby being the centre of the largest ironstone railway system in Northamptonshire, over 60 steam locomotives were shared by the steelworks and quarry traffic during the complex's existence. *(Trevor Riddle)*

INDUSTRIAL ACTION

242. December 1967 and the early morning sunshine highlights the array of semaphore signals on the main Kettering to Manton main line, while an unidentified Hawthorn Leslie locomotive pulls forward with a train of molten slag. In the background another two steam locomotives stand with two diesels as steam and smoke swirl around the buildings at Corby Steelworks. From this vantage point on the Rockingham Road bridge much railway activity could be witnessed, both industrial and BR, and shunting of wagons continued both day and night. *(Trevor Riddle)*

243. In the heart of Corby Steelworks No. 20, a Hawthorn Leslie built 0-6-0ST, stands adjacent to Deene coke ovens on Saturday 13 March 1971. Normally this work would have been carried out by a diesel locomotive but, owing to a failure, No. 20 was rostered for the duty. Red hot coke is discharged into the wagon in front of the locomotive, and is then cooled by water as it is unloaded, creating much steam, as seen in the foreground. The smell and heat from the coke ovens made it a particularly unpleasant duty for the footplate crew on the locomotive. *(Trevor Riddle)*

INDUSTRIAL ACTION

244. All out effort as one of the Robert Stephenson Hawthorn tank engines blasts up a severe incline bringing a train of iron ore into Corby steelworks with smoke and steam in abundance. A dull December's day in 1967 creates the perfect conditions to show the drama of the occasion. Seven of this type of locomotive were purchased in 1950, followed by two others later. They were particularly powerful and no fewer than five were preserved after the closure of the quarries in 1969. *(Trevor Riddle)*

245. No. 3 PEN GREEN, built by Hudswell Clarke in 1903, was one of the oldest locomotives to remain at work at Corby steelworks during the 1960s. The purchase of 'Pen Green' (named after one of the early quarries) in 1903 marked the changeover in policy from four-coupled to six-coupled tank engines for quarry work. This view, photographed in April 1963, shows the locomotive working a train of empty wagons on the railway system, and looking a little worse for wear externally. *(Trevor Riddle)*

246. Smoke to the heavens, as one of the Robert Stephenson Hawthorn locomotives at Corby struggles to move its train of iron ore. The sky over Corby tube works is blackened as the huge plume of smoke hangs in the cold still air of a dull December day in 1967. This is industrial steam at its evocative best! *(Trevor Riddle)*

INDUSTRIAL ACTION

247. More dramatic lighting at Corby, this time to coincide with No. 39 RHOS, a Hudswell Clarke built locomotive working a short engineer's train on the Corby quarries railway system during February 1963. This was one of the locomotives that was kept for quarry use as distinct from use at the steelworks and consequently was kept in immaculate external condition. This is another Corby locomotive that has been preserved. *(Trevor Riddle)*

248. In the depths of Geddington Pit, No. 80, an 0-6-0ST built by Hunslet, struggles to move its train of iron ore on a freezing cold February day in 1964. This spectacular display was quite common during the raw winter months, and very few enthusiasts would have ventured out to witness the display let alone photograph it. The pit was part of the Glendon East quarries system and was situated about two miles north of Kettering. *(Trevor Riddle)*

INDUSTRIAL ACTION

THROUGH THE LANDSCAPE

249. This outstanding panoramic scene from the top of the St Katherine's Court building on Sunday 4 August 1957 gives an excellent view of the landscape looking towards Hunsbury Hill. The briefest of glimpses of Dorridge Street and Chalk Lane in the foreground lead down to St Peter's Church and an array of buildings in Marefair and Black Lion Hill. Many familiar landmarks appear in the picture, most of which have now disappeared, and to complete the scene a 4F class 0-6-0 brings a train into Castle station from Peterborough, having run past the carriage sheds. (W.J.S. Meredith)

250. In direct comparison with the previous illustration, this landscape view is seen from Duston West signalbox looking towards the town showing the St Katherine's Court building vividly standing out on the horizon as the only skyscraper! Sheffield Millhouses Jubilee No. 45664 NELSON ambles up the long climb towards Hunsbury Hill tunnel with its freight train on Sunday 4 June 1961. *(R. Gammage)*

251. Another fascinating panoramic view from the top of the St Katherine's Court building, this time in the direction of St James End on Sunday 4 August 1957. In the foreground are the rooftops of homes in Chalk Lane and Fitzroy Street. Northampton Castle station is on the left, with the station platforms stretching the length of the picture, and the huge railway warehouse in the middle of the view. A 4F class 0-6-0 stands in the platform with a passenger train from Peterborough. The 'Dover' chimney at the cycle works was a landmark in the area, the same way the Express Lifts tower is today! *(W.J.S. Meredith)*

THROUGH THE LANDSCAPE

252. A view from the top of the coaling stage at Northampton locomotive shed during 1964 offered an excellent landscape view of Cotton End. It shows how extensive the railway layout was in this part of the town. On the left the EMEB cooling towers dominate the horizon, while on the right the roofs of the houses in St Leonard's Road lead down to Main Road. A Stanier 8F backs down the line leading to the shed, past Bridge Street Junction signalbox under the familiar footbridge which gave access to the shed from Main Road. Two locomen can be spotted cycling home after finishing their shift. Amazingly, cows graze on the land to the left in this urban scene. *(Brian Bibb)*

253. A superb study of Brackley viaduct on the Great Central, with Annesley Black 5 No. 44665 racing northwards up the 1 in 176 gradient with the 12.32 p.m. (SO) Hastings to Manchester Piccadilly train on 10 August 1963. Earlier the 'Black 5' would have worked light engine from Cricklewood shed to Kensington Olympia where it would have taken over from a Southern counterpart for the trip north. *(Delmi Battersby)*

Two excellent landscape views (on facing page) of the Great Central main line running through the Northamptonshire Uplands on Saturday 3 September 1966, the last day of through passenger services.

THROUGH THE LANDSCAPE

254. *(Top)* 'Black 5' No. 45292 hauls the 16.38 p.m. Marylebone to Nottingham Victoria over Catesby Viaduct on the long 1 in 176 descent from Charwelton. The building in the top right hand side is Catesby House, famous for its association as a meeting place for Guy Fawkes and his fellow collaboraters before their escapades in the Houses of Parliament in London. *(J.N. Simms)*

255. *(Bottom)* 'Black 5' No. 44984, hauling the final southbound service train, the 5.15 p.m. Nottingham Victoria to Marylebone, crosses into Northamptonshire as it storms over Staverton viaduct, with Woodford driver Tom Pavey at the regulator. With a wreath on the smokebox door, and a packed train, the nostalgic journey was successfully completed, watched by many groups of people along the route, and rolled into Marylebone station only a few seconds late. This was quite remarkable considering the rundown condition of locomotives at the time. *(J.N. Simms)*

256. Across a landscape of snow in arctic conditions '15 arches' viaduct stands out as an unidentified class 8F 2-8-0 coasts down the gradient towards Castle station with safety valve blowing, hauling a train of empty coal wagons on the bleak afternoon of Saturday 26 January 1963. Under the larger central arch flowed what was locally known as the 'cut', and an improvised wooden bridge constructed mainly of sleepers can be seen straddling it. This was to enable contractors to carry out strengthening of certain of the arches. The land in the foreground was often flooded after heavy rainfall, being (then, but not now) a flood plain, hence the viaduct instead of a continuous embankment being constructed. (G.R. Onley)

257. A quite remarkable early morning photograph of a northbound freight train on the Great Central railway at Rugby in the 1950s. As the sun gets to work on the dawn mist, rays of light stream through under the arches of the viaduct, creating a truly dramatic effect. The passing of K3 class No. 61856 with its train completes a spectacular and artistic landscape view photographed from near the site of the Rugby Locomotive Testing Plant. *(John G. Click/National Railway Museum)*

THROUGH THE LANDSCAPE

There were so many lines converging on Rugby that a succession of flyovers and underpasses were built in an effort to keep traffic flowing through this bottleneck. Thus a very interesting manmade landscape evolved over the years, especially at the eastern end of the station. A sample of this landscape is shown in the following three views taken in the early 1950s by John Click who worked in the Rugby Testing Station at the time.

258. *(Above)* Rebuilt Patriot No. 45530 SIR FRANK REE on a down Euston to Manchester express, which has been diverted via Northampton, ascends the flyover which takes it over the up main line to Euston, and passes the line from Peterborough sweeping in from the left *(John G. Click/National Railway Museum)*

259. *(Left)* In August 1952 a unique Pacific entered traffic, rebuilt from Sir William Stanier's 'Turbomotive' and named PRINCESS ANNE. Almost brand new No. 46202 is seen heading her down express on the falling gradient towards Clifton Road bridge and the distant Great Central 'birdcage' girder bridge. Steam has already been shut off as the fireman watches for any adverse signals on the station approach. Less than two months later, on 8 October, 'Princess Anne' was damaged beyond economic repair in an accident at Harrow and Wealdstone. *(John G. Click/National Railway Museum)*

260. Photographed from the roof of Rugby Testing Station, a Hawksworth Modified Hall No. 6966 WITCHINGHAM HALL strides purposefully across the Great Central viaduct just north of the 'birdcage' with a Bournemouth to Newcastle express. The 'Hall' will haul the train as far as Leicester, where another locomotive will be waiting to take over for the remainder of the journey northwards. The leading coach is a Gresley brake 3rd, repainted in the 'blood and custard' livery so familiar in the early 1950s. *(John G. Click/National Railway Museum)*

THROUGH THE LANDSCAPE

261. The approach to Roade from Ashton by road offers this rural landscape view of the West Coast main line with the huge water tower in the background, a landmark even today. The tranquillity of a superb midsummer's evening is shattered as Britannia class No. 70032 TENNYSON hurries past with an up-fitted fish train from Fleetwood on Monday 18 June 1962. To local RCTS members, the picture will jog memories as it was taken during one of the society's outdoor meetings during that summer. *(Robin Puryer)*

THROUGH THE LANDSCAPE

262. As the West Coast main line enters the county from the south, the one mile approach to Ashton is built on an embankment. The minor road from Bozenham Mill to Hartwell runs underneath this part of the railway, and it is from this vantage point that rebuilt Royal Scot class No. 46149 THE MIDDLESEX REGIMENT is caught travelling northwards with its express during the autumn of 1959. The photographer's skill with the camera has produced a scene captured to perfection with the locomotive ideally positioned. *(Tony Heighton)*

THROUGH THE LANDSCAPE

263. *(Left)* The signal gantry south of Roade station stands out in the landscape as freezing fog gradually lifts, revealing a Black 5 locomotive involved in engineering duties during the winter of 1960. With steam pressure already above maximum, the fireman takes the opportunity to shovel coal forward in the tender. *(L.H. Cummings)*

264. *(Opposite top)* The river valley at Kingsthorpe Mill is prone to mist and fog during the winter months. The flat landscape north of Northampton No. 5 signalbox is ideally suited to pick out 8F class No. 48736 with its long empty coal train heading towards Market Harborouth on Saturday morning 16 November 1963. As the freezing fog lifts, the thick frost on the ground and the exhaust from the locomotive filling the sky all help to convey a distinctly wintry feeling. *(Robin Puryer)*

265. *(Opposite bottom)* With the gas lamps in the sidings shining brightly in the gathering gloom, an unidentified 'Jubilee' storms southwards with its express to St Pancras during February 1963. Freshly fallen snow has all but covered the running lines, and gathered inches deep on the steps of Kettering South signalbox. This evocative view was photographed from the Headlands Road bridge at Kettering during one of the coldest winters on record. *(Trevor Riddle)*

With Sunday 3 March 1963 being the last day of local passenger services on the Great Central Railway, after which all smaller stations between Aylesbury and Nottingham were closed, these two illustrations show scenes at two of these stations before the end came.

266. On Saturday 2 March 1963 an unidentified 9F class 2-10-0 makes a dramatic appearance at Helmdon with a down freight in the crisp winter air. In the landscape a solitary figure watches the proceedings as the 8.45 a.m. Nottingham to Marylebone semi-fast departs from the station. *(Delmi Battersby)*

267. On Friday 1 March 1963 Woodford Fairburn class 4MT No. 42178 arrives at Finmere station with the 9.08 a.m. Aylesbury to Woodford local stopping train. One passenger with his dog awaits the train on an otherwise deserted platform. In both illustrations the last of the winter's snow melts away, and by 4 March only Woodford and Brackley stations would remain open to passenger trains on the Great Central main line. *(Delmi Battersby)*

THROUGH THE LANDSCAPE

268. An unusual view across the landscape at Woodford Halse with locos standing in the shed yard in the foreground, with an '8F' preparing to leave, and across the marshalling yards houses in Hinton are almost hidden in the winter haze. This rare picture was taken from the top of the shed coaling stage which was some 89 ft in height and dominated Woodford's skyline for several miles and became a local landmark. The date was Sunday 3 March 1963. *(Delmi Battersby)*

269. Glendon North Junction signalbox stands out very well in this landscape view looking north on the Midland main line about three miles north of Kettering station. A class 8F 2-8-0 brings a coal train from the Leicester direction and heads south during the summer of 1959. In the background quarry workings are in evidence. The location used to be a favourite train-spotters site with trains running to and from the Corby direction as well as on the main line through Market Harborough. *(Tony Heighton)*

270. The prospect from the parapet at Blue bridge Glendon gives the railway observer a panoramic view of the four track Midland main line as it leaves Kettering and heads northwards. The chimneys of Kettering Furnaces dominate the background as a freight train is about to be overtaken by a passenger train during the winter of 1965. The '8F' class 2-8-0 heads an empty coal train back to the Nottinghamshire coalfields via Corby and Manton, while the 'Black 5' 4-6-0, hauling a local passenger train to Leicester, uses the direct route via Market Harborough. *(Trevor Riddle)*

THROUGH THE LANDSCAPE

271. *(Top)* The superb Welland Viaduct at Harringworth stretches for almost three quarters of a mile and consists of 82 arches. Harringworth village can just be made out in the background, with the church dominant. It is the longest masonry viaduct across a valley in Britain and has been in existence for 112 years this year, and is still used. The train on the viaduct. is S.R. Lord Nelson class No. 30850 LORD NELSON returning north to Carnforth on Tuesday 31 May 1988. *(Joe Rajczonek)*

272. *(Bottom)* The fireman on board rebuilt Royal Scot class No. 46148 THE MANCHESTER REGIMENT is busy as the locomotive begins to cross the viaduct during the autumn of 1960 with a northbound express. *(Tony Heighton)*

273. (Above) The rural approaches to Roade Cutting on the line from Northampton are well illustrated in this mid-1950s view showing an immaculately groomed combination on the up diverted 'Royal Scot'. The train is headed by Coronation Pacific No. 46227 DUCHESS OF DEVONSHIRE which had received a new smokebox during its May 1953 overhaul to replace the sloping top from previous streamlining as seen on illustration 75. (P.I. Rawlinson)

274. (Below) From the overbridge in illustration 273 we see the view into Roade Cutting looking south-east with Fairburn 2-6-4 tank No. 42106 heading a late afternoon up local 'bunker first' on Friday 10 August 1962. (L. Hanson)

The landscape of Roade Cutting is well represented in these four views of the railway. From a technical point of view, the upper part of the cutting consists of rock which rests on a bed of clay. Under this clay is a bed of loose shale, impregnated with water. Apart from the difficulties of excavating this immense cutting and drawing off the water with steam pumps, was the problem of keeping the sides from falling in. This was dealt with by building the great brick retaining walls now visible on either side. The slow line to Northampton was further reinforced by use of a steel girder structure.

275 and 276. Engineering work on the track comes to a halt to allow a down fitted freight heading for Northampton behind a double-chimneyed class 5 4-6-0 No. 44765 to pass a similar southbound train headed by rebuilt Royal Scot class No. 46169 THE BOY SCOUT. The scene was pictured on a warm sunny Wednesday 29 August 1962. Of interest is the enamel sign on the wall of the cutting showing the way to Northampton some five miles away. One wonders if the sign was erected so that passengers on main line trains that didn't pass through the town were reminded that the town did have a railway station. *(Both pictures: G.R. Onley)*

THROUGH THE LANDSCAPE

L. & N. W. RY.

Daventry

THROUGH THE LANDSCAPE

277. *(Facing page)* A fine bird's eye view of Daventry circa 1950 shows the station and goods yards out on the edge of town. An ex-L.N.W.R. 'Super D' engine stands adjacent to the platform while in the process of shunting the local pick-up freight. Daventry station was situated on the branch line from Weedon to Leamington. Large amounts of chalk were transported along the route from Southam, and this generated a lot of freight traffic to fit in between the local passenger services. The Church of the Holy Cross dominates the picture, while the familiar 'Burton Memorial' stands in the middle of town. In contrast to present times, very few vehicles or pedestrians are to be seen, even at 2.10 in the afternoon. *(Northamptonshire Libraries)*

278. *(Above)* In direct contrast to the previous picture, a view at Olney of splendid isolation as Standard class 2MT No. 84005 scurries off into the landscape with the 2.30 p.m. local train from Northampton to Bedford on Thursday 8 February 1962. Although only a branch line station, an interesting arrangement of sidings can be seen in the vicinity of the signalbox complete with rakes of wagons and other railway vehicles. *(Ken Fairey)*

279. Against the backdrop of a rather industrial looking Northampton, Stanier 8F No. 48122 idles away the time with a Sunday engineering train on 3 November 1963. The train is almost perfectly reflected in the calmness of the River Nene, meandering its way through the rural setting of Foot Meadow. *(L. Hanson)*

THROUGH THE LANDSCAPE

280. Frost lies heavy on the tops of the cars in the station car park at Banbury as dawn breaks during a January morning in 1965. Steam oozes out of the Black 5 and its train, the 9.25 a.m. to Woodford Halse, as the sun tries to appear behind the station building. *(Ian Krause)*

London and South Western Ry.

787

TO

BANBURY

(Via BASINGSTOKE.)

THROUGH THE LANDSCAPE

281. For once conditions are perfect on the morning of Saturday 12 January 1991 as King class No. 6024 KING EDWARD I arrives at Banbury station at 9.45 a.m. with a northbound excursion. The early morning frost is still evident, allowing the locomotive's exhaust to hang motionless in the still air while a gathering of spectators witness the scene. *(Joe Rajczonek)*

282. The sight of a steam locomotive hard at work at night is one of the most dramatic and evocative visual spectacles on the railway scene. To witness the glow of the fire highlighting the footplate crew, the sparks out of the chimney and from spinning wheels as well as the swirling steam and smoke all make up a vivid impression of power. In this landscape view of Banbury station, amid a sea of station lights, King No. 6024 KING EDWARD I makes a stunning sight as it heads south with a return excursion to Paddington on Saturday 7 December 1991. *(Joe Rajczonek)*

283. With the temperature well below zero on a winter's night and not a breath of wind, the exhaust from a southbound steam train fills the night sky in dramatic style. Within half a mile the train would have crossed into Northamptonshire, like a ghost from the past, in this timeless image of steam at night at Banbury. *(Joe Rajczonek)*

INDEX OF LOCOMOTIVES

ALL BRITISH RAILWAYS NUMBERS UNLESS STATED
Numbers in italics are illustration numbers

KEY TO LETTERS INCORPORATED IN LOCOMOTIVE CLASS NUMBERS
P = Passenger; F = Freight; MT = Mixed Traffic (i.e. passenger/freight); T = Tank; WD = War Department; † = Rebuilt with larger tapered boiler

63981, *212*

Gresley 'N2' class 0-6-2T introduced 1920
69583, *195*

G.E.R.

Worsdell 'J15' class 2F 0-6-0 introduced 1883
65390, *226*

G.N.R.

Stirling 2-2-2 7'-7½" single introduced 1885
(Passenger)
G.N. No. 239, *10*

Ivatt class C12 4-4-2T introduced 1898 (Mixed
Traffic)
L.N.E.R. No. 7368, *96*

B.R.

Riddles 'Britannia' class 7P 4-6-2 introduced 1951
70015 APOLLO, *131*
70021 MORNING STAR, *53*
70032 TENNYSON, *261*
70043 LORD KITCHENER, *215*

Riddles 'Clan' class 6P 4-6-2 introduced 1952
72005 CLAN MACGREGOR, *86*

Riddles Standard class 4MT 4-6-0 introduced 1951
75056, *196*

Riddles Standard class 4MT 2-6-0 introduced 1953
76040, *166*
76052, *207*

Riddles Standard class 2MT 2-6-0 introduced 1952
78028, *226*

Riddles Standard class 2MT 2-6-2T introduced 1953
84005, *278*
84007, *51*

Riddles Standard 'WD' class 8F 2-8-0 introduced
1943
90103, *179, 180*
90161, *114*
90190, *142*
90474, *207*

Riddles Standard class 9F 2-10-0 introduced 1954
92025, *216*
92028, *125*
92070, *129*
92087, *130*
92093, *139*
92094, *120*
92095, *140*
92126, *152*
92132, *216*
92153, *120*
92159, *216*

DIESEL TYPES

British Railways Type 4 'Peak' 1Co-Co1 introduced
1959
D49, *188*

English Electric Type 4 1Co-Co1 introduced 1958
D222 LACONIA, *104*
D330, *back end-paper*
D334, *211*
D338, *106*
D372, *105*

North British Shunter 0-4-0 introduced 1958
D2903, *198*

British Railways Type 2 Bo-Bo introduced 1958
D5025, *198*

Birmingham R.C. & W. Co. Type 2 Bo-Bo
introduced 1958
D5395, *175*

L.M.S. English Electric Co-Co introduced 1947
10000, *197*
10001, *197*

L.M.S. and British Railways Shunter 0-6-0
introduced 1945
12089, *156*

Park Royal four-wheel Railbus
M79973, *65*

INDUSTRIAL LOCOMOTIVES

Builder / LOCO NAME/NUMBER	TYPE	CYLIN-DER	MAKER'S No.	YEAR BUILT	GAUGE	
Andrew Barclay Son and Co. Ltd.						
No. 7	0-4-0ST	OC	2135	1941	Standard	*231, 232*
Black, Hawthorn & Co. Ltd.						
KETTERING FURNACES No. 2	0-4-0ST	OC	501	1879	3'-0"	*235*
Hawthorn Leslie & Co. Ltd.						
No. 32	0-6-0ST	OC	3888	1936	Standard	*241*
No. 20	0-6-0ST	OC	3897	1936	Standard	*243*
Hudswell Clarke & Co. Ltd						
No. 3 PEN GREEN	0-6-0ST	IC	607	1903	Standard	*245*
'SHEEPBRIDGE No. 25'	0-6-0ST	OC	431	1895	Standard	*239, 240*
No. 39 RHOS	0-6-0ST	OC	1308	1918	Standard	*247*
Hunslet Engine Co. Ltd.						
No. 80	0-6-0ST	IC	2417	1941	Standard	*248*
Kitson & Co. Ltd.						
No. 44 CONWAY	0-6-0ST	IC	5470	1933	Standard	*238*
Manning Wardle & Co. Ltd.						
KETTERING FURNACES No. 7	0-6-0ST	OC	1370	1897	3'-0"	*234, 236, 237*
Peckett & Sons Ltd.						
No. 85	0-6-0ST	OC	1870	1934	3'-3"	*233*
No. 86	0-6-0ST	OC	1871	1934	3'-3"	*233*
No. 87	0-6-0ST	OC	2029	1942	3'-3"	*230, 233*

L.M.S. 'Royal Scot' class No. 6147.
(The Derby collection/National Railway Museum)